# Angels & Demons

by
Wayne E. Caldwell

Schmul Publishing Co.
Schmul's Wesleyan Book Club Salem, Ohio

Most of the material in this book previously appeared in *A Contemporary Wesleyan Theology*, volume 2, © 1992 Schmul Publishing Company, Salem, Ohio



Published by Schmul Publishing Co.
PO Box 716
Salem, Ohio 44460

Printed in the United States of America

Printed by Old Paths Tract Society
RR2, Box 43
Shoals, Indiana 47581

**ISBN 0-88019-369-7**

# Contents

## *Publisher's Preface*

THERE IS MUCH NONSENSE rampant in our culture today concerning angels. From popular television shows to books in large discount houses, angels are presented to us in highly imaginative form. Usually, they are portrayed as watching over us and protecting us from bad things, rather like some immensely powerful superman with wings. Whether they appear as the angels of Judeo-Christian tradition, or as Hindu *boddhisattvas*, they save us from fires and car wrecks, direct us to lost dogs and money, and help us find the love of our life. But one thing they do not do: they never, never take a judgmental attitude about our lifestyle.

While it is comforting to imagine some benevolent, all-powerful winged Big Brother, invisible and protecting, the modern image of angels is somewhat less than scriptural. When a member of Schmul's Wesleyan Book Club suggested that perhaps the time was right to extract Dr. Caldwell's material on angelology and demonology from SPC's definitive theological publication, *A Contemporary Wesleyan Theology*, we agreed. In a day of confusion, frustration (and sometimes outright saccharine imbecility) the contents of this book provide a clear and orthodox return to firm footing on the subject.

True to his normal form, Dr. Caldwell never takes an obsessive, sensational approach, but insists upon a scriptural treatment on the topic of angels and demons. We offer this book in the assurance that it will provide the concise Wesleyan view of these creatures who play a part in the unfolding history of this fallen planet, imperceptible but potent.

# PART I

## Angelology

# 1

## *Angels: Definition and Delineation*

THE EXISTENCE OF SUPERNATURAL, or heavenly, spiritual beings whose primary purpose is to act as God's messengers to the human family and as agents who do only His will is as certain as every other subject of divine revelation. C. Fred Dickason suggests that "though angelology is not a cardinal doctrine, its acceptance opens the mind to a better understanding of the Bible, God's plan of the ages, the Christian life and ministry, as well as world conditions and course of affairs."[1]

From the oldest records of man's existence, there are depictions of unseen creatures populating aerial spaces. In addition to the nearly universal evidence, there are the profuse and unmistakable references to angels in sacred Scripture. The Bible informs us not only that these spiritual intelligences exist but also that they are divided into two vast hosts: the one active in serving and ministering tot he needs of mankind, the other intent on opposing and defeating God's redemptive plan for the human race, as well as His plans for every high and holy purpose He desires for the universe He has created.

The first host is totally loyal to God and designated by the name *angels*; the second is totally at odds with and in rebellion to God, being under the apostate leadership of Satan, and is designated in the Bible by the name *demons*. The ancient Romans and Egyptians, as well as many contemporary pagans, however, regard certain spirits of departed wicked persons as demons also. It must be borne in mind that much of the biblical data that is to be examined on the subject of angels, whether the good and unsullied angels or the wicked and fallen, is highly symbolic. Like the writers of the scriptural apocalyptic literature, the writers who described angelic beings in their biblical accounts used many figures of speech, and the data must be so interpreted.

Most liberal scholars omit any significant discussion of angels altogether, a fact that indicates their predisposition to ignore biblical revelation at this point. Many who deny, or attempt to deny, the existence of God and the immortality of the soul find no basis at all for the reality of angels. One authority states the case with poignant observation that such scholars "will spend much time in refuting the proofs of the existence of God and the immortality of the soul, but will not even wet the pen to refute the existence of an angelic host."[2]

It seems reasonable, based on the majestically beautiful words of the inspired writer of Hebrews, that the earthly ministry of angels is not only a phenomenon of an earlier dispensation but also one that may well continue to the end of the age. "Are not all angels ministering spirits sent to serve those who will inherit salvation?" (Hebrews 1:14).

In view of the plethora of recent works published on the subject of spirit beings such as angels and demons, it is worthy of note that the editors of *A Contemporary Wesleyan Theology* have given such prominence to the subject treated herewith.

# 2

## *Angels: Scriptural Names, Terms, and References*

IN THE SEPTUAGINT, AS well as the Greek New Testament, *angelos* is the exact equivalent of the Hebrew *malak*, both terms signifying a "messenger." Used to denote the execution of God's purposes or to manifest His presence and power, the Hebrew often connects the names of Jehovah or Elohim with *malak*. The words *kedoshim* in Hebrew and *hoi hagioi* in Greek, meaning "the holy ones," came to be equivalents.

In some passages — such as 1 Samuel 11:3; Job 1:14; Luke 7:4; 9:52 — an ordinary messenger is implied. In other instances *malak* refers to prophets (Isaiah 42:19; Haggai 1:13; Malachi 3:1) and to priests (Ecclesiastes 5:5; Malachi 2:7), and *angelos* used in the New Testament refers to ministers (Revelation 1:20) and to Paul's "thorn in the flesh" ("a messenger of Satan to buffet me" [2 Corinthians 12:7]). Other uses of *malak* include references to impersonal agents, such as the pillar of cloud (Exodus 14:19); pestilence (2 Samuel 24:16-17; 2 Kings 19:30); the winds ("He makes the winds His messengers, flames of fire His ministers," Psalm 104:4); and plagues (Psalm 78:49, where the context is a reminder of the plagues of Egypt as, "a band of destroying angels").

Other expressions used to designate angels collectively are *sodh* ("council"), *edhah* and *kahal* ("congregation"), and *tsabba* or its plural form ("host" or "hosts"). The latter term is by far the most frequently used as in the phrase "God of hosts." It is interesting to note that the Septuagint translates *elohim* in a few places as "angels." The most well-known text where this is done is "Yet thou hast made him little less than God" (Psalm 8:5 RSV), which is quoted in the same version as "lower than the angels" (Hebrews 2:7, 9). Thus, most authorities would agree that the name *elohim*, standing along, never means angels but rather, as in the text cited, "angels of God."[3]

In the New Testament the word *angelos* is used in at least 180 different texts and in all but seven it is translated "angel." In all seven of these exceptions it is translated "messenger" in the King James Version (Matthew 11:10; Mark 1:2; Luke 7:24, 27; 9:52; 2 Corinthians 12:7; James 2:25). When divine messengers are referred to, some phrase makes this very clear, such as "the angels of heaven" (Matthew 24:36) and "a multitude of the heavenly host" (Luke 2:13).

Paul refers to various ranks or grades of supernatural beings in a group of words that are variously combined. These are used in the best sense, as of beneficent beings, in Colossians 1:16, where they are termed "thrones or dominions or rulers or authorities." Here Christ, as Creator, brought "all things" into existence for His own purposes, including specifically these invisible beings. In other passages where these terms appear, they are represented as malignant powers (Romans 8:38; 1 Corinthians 15:24; Ephesians 6:12; Colossians 2:15). In only two references the word *archangelos* ("chief messenger") is used in the Bible — both in the New Testament (1 Thessalonians 4:16; Jude 9).

# 3

## *Angels in the Old Testament*

THERE ARE NO FEWER than thirty-two references to angels in the Pentateuch and thirty-seven in the historical books (Joshua-Esther). In the poetic and prophetic sections of the Old Testament the vast majority of references appear in the Psalms, Isaiah, Daniel, and Zechariah. In quite a number of cases the Angel of the Covenant is identified as the Angel of the Lord or the Angel of Elohim, and sometimes a temporary manifestation of Deity in some form or in conversation is described (*e.g.*, Genesis 18-19; 32:24-28; Exodus 3). Authorities do not agree whether all of these appearances should be interpreted as theophanies, Christophanies, both, or neither.[4]

The angel of the Lord gave comfort to Hagar (Genesis 16:7-13; 21:17). Abraham ate and talked with angels who later delivered Lot, his nephew, from Sodom with his wife and daughters (Genesis 18-19). Jacob dreamed of angels going up and coming down a ladder that reached to heaven (Genesis 28:12); he also wrestled until the break of day with an angel and became crippled (Genesis 32:24-28). Moses was called by the angel of the Lord to lead Israel out of Egypt; an angel also lead Moses and his people through the desert (Exodus 3:2; 14:19; 23:20).

Ruth, 1 Kings, Ezra, Nehemiah, and Esther have no references to angels. The most frequent usage in the historical narratives appears in Judges, where the angel of the Lord spoke with Gideon and with Manoah and his wife (Judges 6:11-24; 13:2-23). David likewise had various experiences with an angel of God, including the loss of many of his people when judgment was administered by an angel after David had taken the army census (2 Samuel 24:1; 1 Chronicles 21).

With the exceptions of Job 4:18; Ecclesiastes 5:6; and Hosea 12:4, all other direct references to angels in the poetic or prophetic sections of the Old Testament are in the Psalms, Isaiah, Daniel and Zechariah. The Psalms present angels as protectors and deliverers of God's people from harm (34:7; 35:5-6; 91:11), as God's devoted servants (104:4), and as fervent worshipers (103:20; 148:2). Isaiah gives two occasions when the angel of the Lord defended Israel and defeated the nation's enemies (37:36; 63:9). He also tells of his remarkable encounter with God in chapter 6, giving a vivid description of the seraphim (the only biblical reference by name to these beings), but he does not specifically call them angels. Jeremiah and Ezekiel do not use the ordinary word for angel, but Ezekiel does refer to the cherubim a number of times (*e.g.*, 10:1-3, 6-8).

The Hebrew children in Babylonian captivity were delivered from the fiery furnace perhaps by an angel (Daniel 3). Daniel himself was spared the agony of death by lions' jaws through an angel sent from God (Daniel 6). Gabriel is first introduced in the Bible when he appeared to Daniel with a revelation of the future of Israel (9:20-27). He later bears messages to Zechariah and Mary (Luke 1). Michael, the archangel of Jude 9, is described in Daniel as one of the "chief princes" (10:13), who resists Israel's enemies and other angelic beings of lesser power (10:13; 12:1). Several of the books of the Minor Prophets and a few other books of the Old Testament have references to messengers of various descriptions, which cannot truly be interpreted as descriptions of angelic beings (Nahum 2:13; Haggai 1:13; Malachi 3:1).

## *The Angel of the Theophany*

One of the most intriguing and mystifying problems of the Old Testament is the usage made of the term "angel of the Lord" which occurs over fifty times throughout the Old Testament in at least ten different books. Some of the texts where this angel appears include those that describe the incident of Hagar's dire plight (Genesis 16:7-13), Abraham's appeal on behalf of Sodom (Genesis 18), the intended sacrifice of Isaac by Abraham (Genesis 22:11ff.); the promise of protection to Eliezer (Genesis 24:7, 40); the angel's appearance to Jacob (Genesis 31:11ff.), Jacob's wresting with the angel (Genesis 32:24ff.); Jacob's blessing of Ephraim and Manasseh (Genesis 48:15-16); the experience of Moses at the burning bush (Exodus 3); the departure of Israel from Egypt (Exodus 13:21; 14:19); the command to the people to obey the angel (Exodus 23:20ff.); Moses' plea for the presence of God for His people (Exodus 32:34-33:17); the appearance of the angel to Joshua (Joshua 5:13-6:2); the angel's speaking to the people (Judges 2:1-5); and the angel's appearance to Gideon (Judges 6:11ff.).

There are occasions when the angel is clearly distinguished from the Lord and at other times, with equal frequency and in the same passages, they are identical or merged together. If the angel in reality is identified with the Lord, then the angel is a theophany, or possibly a Christophany, a manifestation of God in visible, bodily form before the incarnation of Christ.

This angel first appears in the Bible after Hagar fled from Sarai, because she was treated so harshly. By a water spring on the way to Shur, the angel promised Hagar what only God can do: "I will greatly multiply your descendants so that they shall be too many to count" (Genesis 16:10). Moses then records that Hagar "called the name of the Lord who spoke to her, 'Thou art a God who sees'; for she said, 'Have I even remained alive here after seeing Him?'" (Genesis 16:13).

Another occasion that seems incontrovertible with regard to the identification of the "angel of the Lord" with the Lord Himself, is found in Exodus 3, where the angel appeared to Moses "in a blazing fire from the midst of a bush" (3:2). Verse 4 then states that "God called to him from the midst of the bush, and said, . . . 'Do not come near. . . . I am the God of your father, the God of Abraham, the God of Isaac, and the God of Jacob'" (Exodus 3:4-6). Moses, being afraid, had his face and would not "look at God" (3:6).

Without any notice of change of speaker, the record of Gideon's commission also identifies the angel of the Lord with the Lord Jehovah Himself: "And the angel of the Lord appeared to him and said to him, "The Lord is with you, O valiant warrior.' . . . And the Lord looked at him . . ." (Judges 6:12, 14). The conversation that follows shows that Gideon regarded his guest as God Himself. The same is true when Manoah and his wife saw the angel of the Lord and feared they would die because they had seen the Lord (Judges 13:21-22).

In addition to the singular and unique title, "the angel of the Lord," which is on various occasions identified with "the Lord," there are also numerous occasions when the angel is distinctly separate from the Lord. For example, Zechariah 3:1 refers to the angel of the Lord, and verse 2 clearly identifies the speaker as the Lord; yet in Zechariah 1:9-11 a man among the myrtle trees was the angel of the Lord who was to hear the report of horsemen sent by the Lord. Their individual identities are also seen when the angel of the Lord makes intercession for Jerusalem as he speaks to God (vv. 12-13). Likewise the angel of the Lord is pictured by Zechariah as saying, "And the Lord said to Satan, 'The Lord rebuke you, Satan! Indeed, the Lord who has chosen Jerusalem rebuke you!'" (Zechariah 3:2). Thus the angel called the Lord was speaking to the Lord, a rather clear evidence that they are not identical.

Many explanations have been made of the angelic theophanies. Some believe this angel is one with a special commission to carry out some unique plan and purpose of God. Others believe this is a momentary or temporary descent of God into visible bodily form. Still another view, which seems to many authorities most plausible, is the conclusion that this is the divine Logos, with a temporary preincarnated appearance. Although John Wesley does not always specifically apply this interpretation to every passage in which the "angel of the Lord" occurs, he does so in the difficult passages of Zechariah 1 and 3, mentioned above, where he repeatedly identifies the angel as Christ, as well as in many other instances. [5]

One authority summarizes the peculiar operation of God in His various modes of service to the human family as follows:

> In particular providences one may trace the presence of Jehovah in influence and operation; in ordinary angelic appearances one may discover Jehovah present on some side of His being, in some attribute of His character, in the angel of the Lord he is fully present as the Covenant God of His people, to redeem them.[6]

The possibility that the appearance of the angel is a Christophany brings four considerations into focus. They are set forth in the following logical sequence:

> (1) The second person of the Trinity, the Son, is the visible God of the New Testament (John 1:14, 18; Colossians 2:8-0). Accordingly, the Son was the visible manifestation of God in the Old Testament also. (2) The Angel of Jehovah no longer appeared after Christ's incarnation. A reference such as Matthew 1:20 does not identify the angel and should be understood as an angel of the Lord. (3) They both were sent by God and had similar ministries such as revealing, guiding, and judging. The Father was never sent. (4) This angel could not be the Father or the Spirit. They never take bodily form (John 1:18; 3:8). [Matthew 3:16, with parallels in Mark 1:10, Luke 3:22 and John 1:32, may be an exception to this, although the Spirit descending upon Christ as a dove was not in human form.]
>
> The Angel of Jehovah, then, according to all the evidence, seems to be the preincarnate Son. His appearances evidence His eternal existence.[7]

A completely satisfying explanation of this great mystery seems impossible. Our conjectures, even though based on the best biblical evidence, must remain only that. The words of one respected authority are most reassuring:

> It is certain that from the beginning God used angels in human form, with human voices, in order to communicate with man; and the appearances of the angel of the Lord, with His special redemptive relation to God's people, show the working of that Divine mode of self-revelation which culminated in the coming of the Savior, and are thus a foreshadowing of, and a preparation for, the full revelation of God in Jesus Christ. Further than this it is not safe to go.[8]

## *The nature, appearance, and function of angels*

Everywhere in the Old Testament the reality and existence of angels is assumed. Their creation is both implicit and explicit in the words, "Praise the Lord! . . . Praise Him, all His angels; Praise Him, all His hosts! . . . For He commanded and they were created" (Psalm 148:1, 2, 5). When the earth and the universe were created, the angels were already in existence, according to many interpreters, including Adam Clarke and John Wesley in their understanding of Job 38:4, 7.[9]

More than mere influences on the human family, angels are real, spiritual beings. They ate with Abraham, they took Lot by the hand, they accepted hospitality but refused worship. When seen on earth, angels always appeared youthful and quite often majestic, commanding, and awesome. Even when their identity was obscured in such a way that they were thought to be completely human, their bearing called forth the most profound reverence. The power and splendor of their presence was felt by Daniel, the guards around Jesus' tomb, Saul of Tarsus, and others. Jacob was crippled by one touch of an angel's hand. Gideon's offering was consumed by a single stroke of an angel's staff.

It seems more reasonable to conclude that angels may assume physical form, as H. Orton Wiley suggests,[10] than to assert their corporeal subsistence as some authorities do; *e.g.*, "Angels are clothed with ethereal vestures such as St. Paul described in his statement, 'There is a spiritual body' (1 Corinthians 15:44)."[11]

Another writer offers the following line of reasoning:

> Though called spirits (Psalm 109; Hebrews 1:14), this does not prove them to be incorporeal. Man has a spirit (1 Thessalonians 5:23); yet he has a body. That angels have a corporeal nature is rather implied in the words of our Lord, that after the resurrection men shall be like angels (Luke 20:36). It is not more difficult to understand this concerning the angels, than to believe that in their glorified state the redeemed are to exist in "spiritual bodies," as Paul tells us in his great resurrection argument (1 Corinthians 15:44).[12]

Since this question of spirituality as over against corporeality has been an issue of considerable speculation with respect to angels for most of Christian history,[13] no attempt at further solutions will be made at this juncture. What can most assuredly be noted is that angels have *some* of the distinct qualities and attributes of personality, namely, those of intelligence or rationality, of emotion or sensitivity, and of volition or will (the latter being implicit before the defection of Satan, if not at present an attribute of the angelic hosts).

The intelligence of the angels is evidenced in their desire to learn of the salvation of the human race through the preaching of the Gospel: ". . . these things which now have been announced to you through those who preached the gospel to you by the Holy Spirit sent from heaven — things into which angels long to look" (1 Peter 1:12). The great intellectual ability of angels may also be seen in speech communication (Matthew 28:5); in the corruption of wisdom (Ezekiel 28:17); and by the fact that even demons know that Jesus is the Son of God (Mark 1:24, 34) and know the place of their confinement (Luke 8:31). The wisdom or intelligence of the angels is also obviously limited, for they do not know the day and the hour of the Lord's second advent (Matthew 24:36).

Angels also have deep and awesome sensitivity. They were overjoyed at the wondrous creation of God (assuming the traditional view of job 38:7, that "sons of God" is symbolic of the angelic hosts); they gave humble and reverent worship to God, crying "Holy, Holy, Holy" in Isaiah's vision of the Lord (Isaiah 6:3); and there is rejoicing in heaven when even one sinner repents (Luke 15:10).

Created to do the will of God faithfully and intelligently, the will and choice of some angels become opposed to God; and the leader of this rebellion, Lucifer, or Satan, stated his will in five strong "I will" assertions (Isaiah 14:12-15). It is apparent that some of the angels exercised their will to remain loyal to God and others chose to align their wills with Satan's (Matthew 15:41).

It is evident from Scripture that when angels appeared, they most often assumed a human form, for angels were at times mistaken for men (Genesis 18:2, 16: Ezekiel 9:2). There is no reference to an angel appearing in female form, although one passage has been so interpreted (Zechariah 5:9). Most, if not all, biblical and theological authorities conclude that angels are ungendered and that they do not reproduce, procreate, or constitute a race. When Jesus was asked concerning seven brothers who died in rather rapid order, all of them having been consecutively the husband of one woman: "In the resurrection therefore whose wife shall she be?" the Master replied, "In the resurrection they neither marry, nor are given in marriage, but are like angels in heaven" (Matthew 22:27-30).

One of the more familiar subjects in Christian art is that of angels with wings. Both good and evil angels, sometimes imagined as grotesque combinations of human and animal forms, are almost always pictured with wings. The only mention of the seraphim in the Bible (Isaiah 6:2, 6) describes these angelic beings as having six wings, only two of which were used for flight while the other two pairs were used to cover head and feet. The cherubim are also shown to have wings, but only four are mentioned in Ezekiel's description. Their movement is further described as apparently very swift, for they caused a noise like many waters, like an army moving and as a sound from God (Ezekiel 1:5-8, 13-14, 24).

Although it is not specifically stated that Gabriel had wings, he went to Daniel's aid in "swift flight" (Daniel 9:21 RSV). The apostle John also said that he saw "another angel flying in midheaven" (Revelation 14:6). It is probably best to think of the wings as symbolic of rapidity of movement and of fervency to execute God's wishes, rather than as literal physical wings.

This leads us to consider the function of angels and the services they perform. Only vague glimpses of their mode of existence in heaven are given (e.g., 1 Kings 22:19; Isaiah 6:1-3; Daniel 7:9-10; Revelation 6:11), showing them in unending adoration and worship of God. In their ministry to the human race, angels are God's agents of providence, both natural and supernatural, to the body and soul (Exodus 12:23; 2 Samuel 24:16; 2 Kings 19:35; 1 Chronicles 21:16; Psalm 104:4; Acts 12:23; 1 Corinthians 10:10; Hebrews 1:7, 11:28).

In the Book of Genesis there is no mention of angels after the incident of the cherubim being placed at the Garden of Eden until after the call of Abraham. As the history of the chosen family unfolds, the angels at various times, along with the angel of the Lord are seen to mingle with the patriarchs and to watch over their lives. Thus their ministry hallowed domestic life in its trials and blessings alike (Genesis 18-19; 24:7, 40; 28:12; 32:1).

In the later history of the Hebrew nation, angels seem to become increasingly the ministers of wrath and judgment. Angelic appearances are especially concentrated in two periods: those of the judges and the captivity, both of which were periods of transition. In the period of the judges there was little if any direct revelation from the Lord or prophetic guidance, whereas during the captivity there was unusual tribulation and much interaction of God with heathen nations. It should also be noted that in the time of Moses and Joshua there are only a few very obscure references to angels.

In the Book of Judges angels rebuke idolatry (Judges 2:1-4), call Gideon (Judges 6:11), and consecrate Samson to the work of deliverance. But immediately upon the appointment of Samuel, who is generally regarded as the last of the judges and the first of the prophets, angelic appearances cease, the only exceptions being when the prophets or their servants needed specific encouragement themselves (1 Kings 19:5; 2 Kings 6:17). During the prophetic and kingly period angels apparently operated only in the affairs of nature as God's agents. During the captivity, however, while the Jews were constantly in the presence of foreign gods and deities, the angels again gave fresh light and vision to men such as Daniel and Zechariah (Daniel 4:13, 23; 10:10, 13, 20, 21; Zechariah, passim). To work out the purposes of God, these angels not only watched over Jerusalem but also over heathen capitals and kingdoms.

## *The order, rank, and organization of angels*

One of the most striking facts stated repeatedly in various ways in Scripture is that the angels are innumerable. Daniel 7:10 mentions "thousands upon thousands" and "myriads upon myriads," or "a thousand thousands" and "ten thousand times ten thousands" (RSV) of angelic beings with the "ancient of Days," all prepared for conflict. Jesus stated that there were "twelve legions of angels" (Matthew 26:53) at His disposal when He was arrested in the Garden of Gethsemane; a "multitude of the heavenly host" (Luke 2:13) gave praise to God at the birth of Jesus; and "innumerable angels in festal gathering" (Hebrews 12:22 RSV) or "myriads of angels" (NASB) are pictured as gathered on Mount Zion, "the heavenly Jerusalem."

Underscoring the pictures of vast numbers of angels in both Testaments is the expression "Lord of Hosts" (or "Jehovah God of Hosts), used no fewer than 280 times in the Old Testament. They are represented as standing on the right and left hand of God (1 Kings 22:19) and they have the principal duty and occupation of praising the name of the Lord (Psalm 103:21); 148: 1-2). Among the massive number of angels certain ones stand out prominently, and some of them are named, as noted, such as Gabriel (Daniel 9:21; 8:15) and Michael (Daniel 10:13, 21; 12:1). In apocryphal literature the names of Raphael, Uriel, and Jeremiel are used, Raphael being identified as one of the "seven holy angels who present the prayers of the saints" to God (Tob. 12:15), a statement that some authorities have identified with the statement of John (Revelation 8:2).

It is interesting to note that early and medieval theologians built a complex hierarchical, even if speculative, structure and description of the angelic world. Pseudo-Dionysus, probably the most original thinker on the subject of angels, arranged them into three ascending or descending orders or groups of nine choirs. Aquinas followed this lead and also projected three hierarchies, but his main interest was in the "nature of angels as individuals" and as "spatial, spiritual substances engaged primarily in the work of enlightenment and capable of rational demonstration."[14]

The question of angelic orders is actually raised by the two enumerations found in Paul's letters to the Ephesians and the Colossians, where "rule and authority and power and dominion" (Ephesians 1:21) or "thrones or dominions or rulers or principalities" (Colossians 1:16) are thought to be references to angels. Thus Dionysus the Pseudo-Areopagite in *Celestial Hierarchies* fixed the three choirs in each of three hierarchies as (1) Seraphim, Cherubim, and Thrones; (2) Dominions, Virtues, and Powers; and (3) Principalities, Archangels, and Angels. Only the last two choirs had any immediate mission to people, according to Dionysus.[15] It should be understood that such speculative ordering is transparently artificial, although intriguing.

Billy Graham believes the order and ranking of celestial powers is conjectural but gives his own conjectured order in terms of authority and glory: archangels, angels, seraphim, cherubim, principalities, authorities, powers thrones, might, and dominion — as based on such Scriptures as Genesis 3:24; Exodus 25:18; Psalms 80:1; 99:1; Isaiah 6:1-6; Ezekiel 9:3; 10:5; Daniel 8:16; 9:21; 10:21; Luke 1:9, 26; Romans 8:38; Colossians 1:16; 1 Thessalonians 4:16; 1 Peter 3:22; Jude 9.[16]

On the other hand, some authorities believe that the cherubim are "angelic beings of the highest order or class, created with indescribable powers and beauty,"[17] and that below them in rank are the seraphim, the living creatures or beasts of Ezekiel 1, followed by those with names — *i.e.*, Michael and Gabriel — followed by other designations of uncertain order.[18]

Still another writer lists the names of groups such as thrones, lordships, principalities, authorities, angels, and powers, then states that "thrones are greater than lordships; and principalities are apparently higher than authorities," with the further comment that "it would seem from previous use of the terms, that thrones and dominions (lordships) refer to good angels, while principalities and powers (authorities) refer to bad angels."[19]

The only appropriate approach to the question of order, rank, and organization is to recognize that in the Bible God, as the supreme and absolute Person of order and authority, has given varying descriptions of angelic beings with different responsibility and activity fulfilled in an obedient purposeful manner at appropriate intervals of history. Thus the cherubim are stationed with flaming swords at the gate of the Garden of Eden to protect the way to the tree of life, teaching that sin and paradise are incompatible (Genesis 3:24); they appear over the mercy seat in the tabernacle, which designates the dwelling place of God in the midst of Israel (Exodus 25:17-22); they appear in prophetic vision as polished brass or bright coals of fire with movements flashing like lightning (Ezekiel 1:7, 13-14); and they seem to have as their main purpose and activity the protection of God's sovereignty, holiness, and glorious presence.

Related closely to the cherubim are the seraphim, whose chief duty is to praise and proclaim the perfect holiness of God. Their name means "burning," thus it is fitting that they are pictured in Isaiah 6 as being aflame with adoration to the holy God. The threefold ascription of "Holy" in the trisagion has always been interpreted as indicating the perfection of holiness, usually of the threefold personage of the Godhead. The priestly role is also a distinguishing feature of the seraphim, in that they announce man's need for cleansing and purification before he can stand before a holy God and serve Him.

We may conclude, therefore, that specific information is given in the Old Testament concerning such groups as the cherubim and seraphim, as well as individuals, *i.e.*, Michael and Gabriel. But beyond that, besides what is generally stated of angelic activity, we have little knowledge and can only speculate as to numbers, rank, and organization.

# 4

## *Angels in the New Testament*

ANGELS APPEARED AT CRUCIAL times in the New Testament as well as in the Old. At strategic times such as the births of John the Baptist and Jesus, the Resurrection, and times of great persecution or emergency, angels of various numbers and descriptions bore special messages of direction, guidance, or announcement. At no time and on no occasion is there the slightest inconsistency between the two Testaments, separated as they are by several centuries.

### *Their existence and appearance*

The angel Gabriel, who alone is named in the birth narratives of the Gospels,[20] appeared to Zacharias (Luke 1:19), declaring that even though he was an old man he would have a son. Approximately six months later, Gabriel was sent by God to Nazareth in Galilee to inform Mary that she was to be the mother of a son, whose name was to be Jesus (Luke 1:26ff.). Meanwhile, an unidentified angel appeared to Joseph (Matthew 1:20), reassuring him that the child to be born to Mary was conceived by divine engenderment. Again, on two separate later occasions, an unidentified "angel of the Lord" appeared to Joseph, telling him when to go to Egypt for the protection of Jesus from Herod and when to return to Israel (Matthew 2:13, 19).

Although Luke does not mention the angelic visits to Joseph, he stays close to the heartbeat of Mary and records the announcement of the birth of Jesus by "an angel of the Lord" (Luke 2:9), along with other tidbits of interesting data. He also notes the "multitude of the heavenly hosts" (Luke 2:13) that join the announcing angel in a mighty, glorious song of praise to God.

Matthew makes a point to relate that after Jesus' temptation in the wilderness angels came and ministered to Him (Matthew 4:11). Likewise, Luke tells of an angel who came and strengthened Jesus prior to His agony, when He prayed more fervently and sweat drops like blood (Luke 22:43-44).

All four Gospel writers record the appearance of angels at the empty tomb of Jesus, although their accounts vary as much as the people who visited the tomb. Matthew writes that an angel of the Lord rolled the stone away (28:2), and as he sat on the stone "his appearance was like lightning, and his garment as white as snow" (28:3-7). In Mark's Gospel, there is "a young man sitting at the right, wearing a white robe" (16:4), to the amazement of the early-morning visitors. Luke states that "two men suddenly stood near . . . in dazzling apparel" (24:4-7). He also records the fact that on the road to Emmaus later the same day it was reported "some women" had seen "a vision of angels" (24:22-23). John writes that Mary Magdalene saw "two angels in white sitting, one at the head, and one at the feet, where the body of Jesus had been lying" (20:12).

It is significant that Luke has many references to angels and their ministry in his New Testament history. At the ascension of Christ, two angels announced His second advent (Acts 1:10-11); an angel of the Lord opened the doors and freed the apostles when they were in prison (Acts 5:19); and an angel of the Lord directed Philip to a desert road running from Jerusalem to Gaza, where he encountered the Ethiopian eunuch and led him to Christ (Acts 8:26-39). An angel of God appeared to Cornelius in a vision and told him to send for Peter to learn the way of salvation (Acts 10:1-7). Peter was freed by an angel of the Lord after Herod Agrippa I had him cast into prison. Then when Peter went to the home of

Mary, mother of John Mark, where a prayer meeting for his release was being held, they couldn't believe it was Peter and concluded it was "his angel" (Acts 12:1-16). The same Herod, soon after the release of Peter, was stricken by an angel of the Lord "because he did not give God the glory, and he was eaten of worms and died" (Acts 12:23). Finally, on his voyage to Rome, Paul was visited by an angel, who assured him that all lives on board the ship would be spared (Acts 27:23-26).

## *The teaching of Jesus concerning angels*

Jesus Christ testified to the existence and reality of angels. He substantiated the Jews' beliefs and the main teachings of the Old Testament, as well as the later concepts concerning both good and evil angels. He did not simply accommodate Himself to prevalent views as some have concluded, for if He spoke of angels just because the people of His day thought they were real, while all the time He knew there were no such beings, He would have been perpetuating an untruth, which as the Son of God He could never do.

In Matthew's Gospel, Jesus taught His disciples to pray that the Father's will would be done on earth as it is in heaven (6:10), implying the obedience of those who reside in heaven now. He said that angels would separate the righteous and the wicked at the end of the age (13:39-44, 49); and when speaking of children as an example of humility, Jesus said their angels in heaven continually behold the face of his Father in heaven (18:1-10). In connection with the teaching that angels are ungendered and that the human race would be like that in heaven, Jesus also spoke of heaven as the home of angels (22:30). Furthermore, Jesus stated that the angels, though intelligent, did not know the day or the hour of His second coming (24:30); they will, however, accompany Christ at that event (25:31). The devil and his angels will be cast into a fire prepared for them (25:41). Jesus said He could have summoned more than twelve legions of angels to help Him in the Garden of Gethsemane (26:53).

In summary, we may conclude that Christ gave ample evidence for the existence of both good and evil angels; that the angels are intelligent and powerful, though generally invisible; and that they work to our benefit, or in the case of the wicked angels, to our woe.

## *The teaching of the epistles and the Book of Revelation*

References to angels in the epistles include at least thirty distinct uses, with nearly half of these occurring in the Book of Hebrews. In the Apocalypse there are no fewer than sixty-five clear usages of the Greek angelos, referring to spirit beings either symbolizing human messengers or referring in reality to God's personal emissaries.

Angels are classified either as elect (1 Timothy 5:21) or as fallen and wicked (2 Peter 2:4). They are living, real beings placed in juxtaposition to Christ, the living Savior. Paul warned the Colossians not to worship angels and seems to declare the defeat of evil angels when he refers to "rulers and authorities" (Colossians 2:15, 18). Peter also speaks of the defeat of evil beings by the triumph of Christ over "authorities and powers," which are subject to Him (1 Peter 3:18-22). Paul may refer to the same fact in Ephesians 1:20-21. Paul, Peter, and James all agree, however, that Christ is the only power strong enough to overcome and defeat Satan and his allies (Ephesians 6:10-12; James 4:7; 1 Peter 5:8-9).

Paul taught that the angels will be judged by the saints (1 Corinthians 6:3) and he commanded women to keep their heads covered in church "because of the angels" (1 Corinthians 11:10).[21] Paul held the angels in highest regard because the law was "ordained through angels by the agency of a mediator" (Galatians 3:19). And, writing to Timothy, Paul states in the "common confession" that Christ was seen by angels, apparently with reference to the many occasions when they ministered to Him in His earthly life (1 Timothy 3:16).

In the Book of Hebrews, the angels are shown to be of lesser ability and power, since Christ has a more excellent name than they (1:4), the angels have never been called a "Son" (1:5), the angels of God worship Christ (1:6), and God has never invited any of the angels to sit on His right hand (1:13). Furthermore, the angels are described as "winds" and as a "flame of fire" (1:7), and they are "all ministering spirits, sent out to render service for the sake of those who will inherit salvation" (1:14).

Moreover, the writer of the Book of Hebrews states that the word of the angels is steadfast and "unalterable" (2:2); the world to come will not be subject to them (2:5); mankind is for a while lower than the angels (2:7); and Christ did not give Himself for the benefit of angels, but for Abraham and his seed (2:16). The only other references to angels in Hebrews occur in the last two chapters. They are described as an innumerable company (12:22), and believers are exhorted to hospitality, for some have "entertained angels without knowing it" (13:2).

With the exception of those references to "messengers" (meaning pastors or human spiritual leaders) in the letters to the seven churches, all other references in the Apocalypse seem to be made to spirit beings used by God to bring about His will and purpose at the end of the age. Even a cursory study of the last book of the Bible reveals a beautiful panorama of the heavenly helpers and, by horrible contrast, the desperate, terrible fate of those taken by evil spirits or by devils.

In the Book of Revelation, which contains more direct references to angels than any other book of the Bible, the angels are portrayed as worshiping the Lamb of God (5:11-12), preserving the saints in the midst of great trial and tribulation (7:1-3), and administering the wrath of God on disobedient and rebellious unbelievers (Revelation 8, 9, 15, 16).

Finally, the pictures in the Apocalypse include the mention of angels who are given specific charge of various elements, *viz.*, "the angel of the waters" (16:5); the "angel, the one who has power over fire" (7:1); the angel who stood in the sun and cried "to all the birds which fly in midheaven" that they should assemble for the great supper of God (19:17); and the angel that has the "key of the abyss" (20:1).

It may also be noted that John received the command that he should not worship the angel who had shown him the preceding prophecy (22:8-9). Thus we may conclude that at the end of the age, as revealed to John, there will be increased activity on the part of the angels of God and that without their aid, mankind would not be properly served, either in respect to their punishment or in respect to their preservation and reward.

# 5

## *The Development of a Doctrine of Angelology*

THE THEME OF ANGELOLOGY is one that is extremely fascinating and enticing to the imagination. Thus at times popular thought has outrun the data base of revelation. This was true in Judaism also, with special respect to the Old Testament Apocrypha and later Jewish literature.

Three or four periods may be distinguished in the progress of biblical angelology. In the preliterary prophetic era, from Abraham to Amos, angelic visitations are described at varying intervals. Most, if not all, of the heavenly messengers appear as agents of the Lord with temporary, but specific, commissions.[22] They bear no titles or special ranks.

During the literary period of prophetic utterance, prior to the exilic era, there is little advance in concept or expression regarding angels. The function of angels is not stressed because there was a direct mediatorial link between God and Israel through the faithful prophets, who needed no intervention of heavenly beings. During the period of the Exile angels became conspicuous as bearers of divine messages. Also at that time there appear distinctions by name and rank among the angels, and in general a more developed angelology becomes evident.

Contact with Persian thinking is sometimes suggested as the explanation of such a development, but this seems most unlikely. The interior understanding based on the supernatural revelation of the Lord Himself to the Jews, seems a more likely conclusion. The New Testament assuredly may not multiply accounts of visible appearances of angels, but it does broaden the foundation for an enlarged concept of the angels' invisible agency.

From the various statements about the nature and work of angels, early and medieval theology built up a very complex and speculative description of the angelic world. Pseudo-Dionysus, though of uncertain identity, proved to be the most original and constructive thinker in this field. He is the person who believed the angels belonged in ascending or descending groups of nine choirs each, as previously noted.

Thomas Aquinas, the "angelic doctor," also treated this question with great alacrity and comprehensiveness. He posited three hierarchies but centered his primary interest in the nature of angels as individuals. He concluded they were "spatial spiritual substances engaged primarily in the work of enlightenment" and that they were "capable of rational demonstration."[23]

Although the Roman Catholic doctrine of angels is probably indebted to the pseudonymous Greek writings of Dionysus the Areopagite, through the Latin rendering of John Erigena,[24] there has been a great deal of additional unscriptural elaboration of the subject by later writers, and this has prompted widespread abuse of the subject. Augustine thought the different ranks of angels should be defined by the diverse functions they practice. He further stated that all material existences, including man himself, were governed by the "reasoning spirit of life," and therefore the angels, being of higher order, were responsible in diverse ways for the affairs of the human race. Gregory the Great also concluded that "in this world of visible things nothing can take place save through the agency of invisible things."[25]

The Council of Trent, furthermore, taught that angels make intercession for people and that it is good and profitable to invoke them suppliantly for the purpose of obtaining benefits from God through His Son, Jesus Christ.[26]

Orthodox Protestant views are copiously quoted by Heppe[27] and more accurately follow familiar biblical lines. Thus, although angels have everlasting existence (1 Timothy 6:16), they were created *ex nihilo* and therefore lack true eternity, which is a prerogative of deity alone and must be retrospective as well as anticipatory. Although angels are finite and therefore limited spirits, they do possess powers that far surpass those of human beings, whose knowledge is limited to nature, experience, and revelation of supernatural weight.

John Calvin correctly evaluated much of the angelological speculation as erroneous in that it treated angels in abstract rather than biblical terms. Even with respect to the function of angels, there was a tendency to concentrate and rationalize their work as a guardianship of the human family. The inevitable result came in the age of the Enlightenment and in the onset of liberal Protestantism, when angels were either summarily dismissed as ridiculous and fantastic or subjected to a "thorough-going neologization."[28]

Two examples of such diverse positions will serve to show this development. The first example, by Martensen, is as follows:

> Schleiermacher is of the opinion that there is no essential difference between the belief in angels and the belief in the existence of rational beings in other planets, inasmuch as the angels owe their origin to no other source than the necessity which man feels for peopling the universe with rational beings different from himself. But this manner of regarding the subject rests upon an utterly erroneous conception of the nature of angels. For even if we accept the very doubtful hypothesis, that there are also inhabitants upon the other heavenly bodies, we can only imagine them to ourselves as in some measure analogous to man, consequently as rational beings, whose existence is a certain form of union of body and spirit; and these individuals, therefore, will again require angels, and stand under the influence of universal powers. On every heavenly body in which we imagine a human race to exist, the metaphysical opposition between heaven and earth will manifest itself, and consequently the opposition between a human life moving on in a succession of historical events, and

> whose universal powers and energies of Providence to which human life stands in a certain relation, will be apparent.[29]

On the other hand, Bultmann explains away the existence of angels — at least belief in their existence — as follows:

> From the time that we have known of nature's power and laws, belief in spirits and demons has been extinguished. The stars appear to us as bodies which form part of the world, and the movement of which is regulated by cosmic laws. . . . Diseases and their cure have natural causes, and are not caused by the action or rather the bewitching of demons. . . . We cannot make use of the electric light and the radio, or in case of illness employ modern medical methods and treatment, and at the same time believe in the world of spirits and the miracles of the New Testament. Anyone who thinks he can do so for himself should realize that, if he claims this as the position of the Christian faith, he renders the Christian message incomprehensible and impossible for our times.[30]

The place that must be assigned to angels and other spirit beings will show how excessive and exaggerated such positions have been. Sometimes clever people of a modern frame of mind simply keep quiet about this subject in order, as they think, to render the Gospel more acceptable. Perhaps it is not possible for modern generations to think of angels with the simplicity and subtlety of ancient peoples, but we can never deny the claim that faith places on us at any difficult juncture of theology.

# 6

## *The View of John Wesley*

IN THIS SERMON ON *the Discoveries of Faith,* based on Hebrews 11:1, John Wesley asserts that, like the souls of men, there are "other orders of spirits: yea I believe that 'Millions of creatures walk the earth unseen, whether we wake, or if we sleep.' "[31]

Wesley further stated that these "angels" were both good and evil, that is to say, "part of them are holy and happy, and the other part wicked and miserable."[32] The good angels continually minister to the heirs of salvation, who are presently inferior to the angels but will become equal to the angels.

In his *Roman Catechism* Wesley includes the angels along with Mary, the saints, and the "blessed Trinity" as objects of worship in the "Church of Rome." Wesley points out that only God is to be worshiped (Matthew 4:10) and that it is unlawful to worship any other being or thing. The Catholics are aware of this but claim they do not give the same kind of worship to angels and to the saints as they do to God.

Wesley queries, "What honor do they give to the angels?" to which his reply is:

> The Church of Rome teaches that angels are to be worshiped, invoked, and prayed to. And they have litanies and prayers composed for this purpose. . . . They teach, that as every particular person hath a guardian angel from his birth, so it is fit to commit themselves more particularly to him, after this manner:

> Blessed angel! To whose care our loving Creator hath committed me, defend me this day, I beseech you, from all dangers, and direct me in the way I ought to walk. (*The Child's Catechism*, 1678)[33]

Wesley comments further as follows:

> We honor the holy angels, as they are God's ministers, and are "sent forth to minister unto them that shall be heirs of salvation." (Hebrews I. 14) But, to worship or pray to them we dare not, as it is what they themselves refuse and abhor, (Revelation xix. 10) and the Scripture doth condemn as "a sign of a fleshly mind, vainly intruding into those things which we have not seen." (Colossians ii. 18.) Theodoret, upon this text, saith, that the practice of worshiping angels continued a long time in Phrygia and Pisidia; wherefore the Synod of Laodicea doth forbid praying to angels: "For Christians ought not to forsake the church of God, and depart aside and invocate angels, which are things forbidden." (Conc. Laod., can. 35)[34]

Wesley's Sermon LXXI, *Of Good Angels*, is based on Hebrews 1:14, "Are they not all ministering spirits, sent out to render service for the sake of those who will inherit salvation?" In it he observes that many heathen people had ideas of both good and evil spirit beings of a superior order. Their concepts of both categories were "crude, imperfect, and confused," since they were based on fragmented truth gathered partly from tradition and partly from inspired writers. The "demon of Socrates" was of the benevolent variety and was supposed to give daily advice as to the evil that might befall his person during the day.

Wesley interprets Hebrews 1:14 as giving strong affirmation to the existence of angels. His further observation continues in the following manner:

> With regard to their essence, or nature, they are all spirits; not material beings; not clogged with flesh and blood like us; but having bodies, if any, not gross and earthly like ours, but of a finer

> substance; resembling fire or flame, more than any other of these lower elements. And is not something like ours, but of a finer substance; resembling fire or flame, more than any other of and his ministers a flame of fire?" (Psalm civ. 4.) As spirits, he has endued them with understanding, will, or affections, (Which are indeed the same thing; as the affections are only the will exerting itself various ways) and liberty. And are not these, understanding, will, and liberty, essential to, if not the essence of, a spirit?[36]

Caught up in wonder and inspiration, Wesley exults in the understanding and wisdom that angels must have. Human language is inadequate for Wesley to imagine the superlative degree to which angels have advanced over the course of "more than six thousand years! What measures of holiness, as well as wisdom, have they derived from the inexhaustible ocean!"[37]

Considering the fact that even a fallen angel is designated "the prince of the power of the air," Wesley reasons that all angels have great power and strength. He is especially taken up with the ability they have to exercise power over the human body, "either to cause or remove pain and diseases, either to kill or to heal." In support, Wesley alludes to Job who was smitten with severe boils and would have been killed had not the Lord prevented it. On the other hand, Daniel was left without strength or breath, after his vision described in chapter 10. But he was given unusual strength when Michael touched him.

Furthermore, angels are so fully qualified for their work of ministering to the heirs of salvation that, for Wesley, they assist in the search for truth, they warn of evil in disguise, they may quicken one's dull affections, they may prevent a person from falling into danger, and when "a violent disease, supposed incurable, is totally and suddenly removed, it is by no means improbable, that this is effected by the ministry of an angel."[38]

Although the ministry of angels is primarily to the heirs of salvation, to those who are "saved by faith," Wesley does not rule out the hope and possibility that angels also seek out the obstinate and the impenitent. Moreover, angels also deliver the just and holy believer from evil men and their devices as well as counteract the work of evil angels. Here Wesley draws on the biblical injunction to beware of wicked angels who go about as roaring lions, or "more dangerously still, as angels of light."[39]

Wesley makes yet another observation: God does not always by His own immediacy come to the aid of His family. He reasons that if God works His will by people to people, to give light in the midst of darkness, joy in heaviness, deliverance when in danger, ease and health when sickness and pain strike, then it may be assumed that God does all these things and more on a higher level and to a greater degree by His holy angels. Wesley continues with these words:

> The grand reason why God is pleased to assist men by men, rather than immediately by himself, is undoubtedly to endear us to each other by these mutual good offices, in order to increase our happiness both in time and eternity. And is it not for the same reason that God is pleased to give his angels charge over us? Namely, that he may endear us and them to each other, that by the increase of our love and gratitude to them, we may find a proportionable increase of happiness, when we meet in our Father's kingdom.[40]

Some of Wesley's concluding remarks in Sermon LXXI include the following poem from the pen of Bishop Ken, with an added prayer of his own, as follows:

> *O may thy angels, while I sleep,*
> *Around my bed their vigils keep;*
> *Their love angelical instill,*
> *Stop every avenue of ill!*
> *May they celestial joys rehearse,*
> *And thought to thought with me converse!*[41]

> O everlasting God, who has ordained and constituted the services of angels and men in a wonderful manner; grant as thy holy angels

> always do thee service in heaven, so by thy appointment they may succor and defend us on earth, through Jesus Christ our Lord.[42]

In showing what Christian perfection is not, in his sermon *On Perfection*, Number LXXVI, Wesley is certain that believers do not have the perfection of angels and that the writer of Hebrews doe not so intend his words "Let us go on unto perfection" (6:1 KJV). The angels who kept their first estate did not decline from their original perfection; their native faculties remain unimpaired, their understanding is still a lamp of light, their judgment is true, and their apprehension of all things is clear and distinct. Therefore, because of the fall of man and his present state of corruptibleness, no human being in this life can possibly attain to angelic perfection.[43]

# 7

## *Guardian Angels*

OF SPECIAL INTEREST TO Roman Catholic theology is the belief in guardian angels. This subject is mentioned here to indicate the extent to which the idea of guardian angels flourished among the church fathers, an idea that continues today among various groups in addition to the Roman Catholic church. Thomas Aquinas cites such churchmen as Jerome, Gregory, Chrysostom, Origen, and Augustine, who taught that the work and ministry of guardian angels included assignment to each person of the human family.[44]

Regamey also cites numerous authorities in addition to church councils that have spoken to the subject. He states that Clement of Alexandria, Tertullian, and Origen all agreed that only Christians had guardian angels and that they were assigned at one's baptism. On earth, only Christ did not have such an angel, for He was supreme over all, being the divine Word Himself. One witness shows the extent of such belief during the early Christian era, as follows:

> I have an amazing guardian angel; he is more cunning than myself! I am protected, and cannot escape him. Three times I have felt him seize me, and snatch me from what I wanted to do, from acts I had planned and determined. His tricks are incredible.[45]

Some early writers in Christendom even believed that each person had two angels, one good and the other evil. It is so indicated in the following quotation:

> A man has two angels: an angel of justice, and an angel of evil. The angel of justice is tender, reserved, sweet and peaceful. When he comes to your heart he speaks at once to you of justice, holiness, temperance and every right work. When these thoughts rise in your heart, know that the angel of justice is with you. The angel of evil, on the other hand, is quick to anger, full of bitterness and madness. Know him by his works. . . . Do not fear the devil. . . . He can only frighten you, but it is an empty fear, do not fear him, and he will flee from you. . . . He cannot rule over the servants of God, who put all their hope in God. He can fight but not conquer. So, if you resist him, he will flee away from you.[46]

The belief that God assigns to every person an angel to guard him in body and soul was common to pagan and Jewish thought. As we have seen, this belief was generally accepted also by the church fathers, but the first clearly defined material may have been projected by Honorius of Autun, who died in 1151. He held that each soul was entrusted to an angel at the moment it was introduced into the body. No true consensus was possible, but the angelic care was generally thought to begin at conception.[47]

Muslims and some Jewish authorities maintain similar views today. Luther Lee wisely states, "The doctrine that every person has a guardian angel may be true, but there is insufficient evidence in Scripture to substantiate the teaching."[48]

The Scriptures that are most frequently mentioned as support for the idea of guardian angels are Psalm 34:7, "The angel of the Lord encamps around those who fear him, and delivers them"; Psalm 91:11, "For he will give his angels charge of you to guard you in all your ways"; Matthew 18:10, "See that you do not despise one of these little ones; for I tell you that in heaven their angels always behold the face of my Father who is in heaven"; and Acts 12:15. In the last passage we are told that

Peter stood at the door knocking and when Rhoda tried to convince those praying for Peter in the home of John Mark's mother, Mary, that it was Peter, they said, "You are mad." When she persisted, they said, "It is his angel."[49]

It seems most reasonable to conclude that God does give responsibility to His angels in various ways for the "heirs of salvation," and that since children are sometimes despised and forsaken, even by their parents, Christ teaches that His Father regards them so highly that He includes them in various ministries by His "ministering spirits," the angels. This does not imply, necessarily, that each child has a guardian angel. It would be too much to infer from a rather obscure text what may be simply a fanciful opinion.

# 8

## *Angelology: A Summary for Contemporary Consideration*

THE EXISTENCE OF ANGELS; how and when they originated; as well as what we may know of their nature, purpose, and work and of their character, rank, organization, or classification is purely a matter of revelation. All that we may know of the angels we must learn from the Scriptures. Anything other than this may be interesting and intriguing but must be understood as conjecture and speculation. And, as Miley states:

> The words of Scripture respecting the angels cannot be reduced to a merely figurative sense, nor to the meaning of mere things in the providential use of God, nor yet to mere forms of his personal energizing. In the clear light of the Scriptures the angels are realities of personal existence. That such was the faith of the Jews in the time of our Lord is above questions.[50]

Both Christ and Paul were allied against the Sadducees in the latter's denial of angelic reality and it is utterly groundless to assume that Christ or Paul spoke in favor of angelic reality only to accord with popular belief. In logical sequence, therefore, we may note what is implicit if not explicit in Scripture, as follows:

### *Angels are created beings*

It is clearly implied in Scripture that angels are neither infinite nor eternal, otherwise they would be equal with God. Although they have spiritual essence, they are finite and temporal beings, commanded by God to worship, praise, and adore Him.[51] Many scholars draw the conclusion that angels were created long before man, the earth, or the universe; however, the Scriptures are silent as to when the angels came into existence. Assuredly the cherubim were sent to guard the way to the tree of life after the fall of Adam and Eve, and some authorities believe that Job 38:6-7 is a figurative reference to the angels. Thus "most people would agree, whether or not they believe these words in Job [refer to angels or celestial bodies], that if there are angels at all, they were probably in existence before man."[52]

### *Angels are spirit beings, sometimes referred to as "pure spirit"*

The phrase "pure spirit" implies that angels are free from material substance. This is not to disparage matter or to identify it with evil, as the Gnostics do. The activities of angels suggest they are spirit-beings, and this view of their spirituality is the nearly unanimous understanding of scholars. The luminous appearance of angels in some instances, together with the difficulty of understanding their activity without a body, has led some to the position that their bodies are ethereal without self-manifesting quality. Visibility, therefore, is completely voluntary or optional.

It seems true to revelation that angels do not have a material fleshly body, such as humans have. This follows from Hebrews 1:14, which states they are "ministering spirits." It may be that angels do have some kind of body, which is not known to us now but is similar to the human resurrected body called by Paul a "spiritual body" (1 Corinthians 15:44).

The council of Nicea, A.D. 787, declared that angels had bodies of ether or light. The Lateran Council, A.D. 1215, declared that angels are incorporeal.[53] The rather common faith of so many varied voices, that angels have no material form, at least as we know it, seems true to revelation. But, as they have often done

(Matthew 1:20; Luke 1:26; John 20:12; Hebrews 13:2), angels are able to assume physical form and shape.

## *Angels have freedom of appearance and have many varied forms*

While angels are normally invisible (Colossians 1:16), they have the unusual ability to make themselves visible, subject to the will of God (Luke 1:11-13, 26-29). Angels appeared in dreams as to Joseph (Matthew 1:20). They were also disclosed in visions, such as to Isaiah (6:1-8). Isaiah's vision focused on God Himself, but the vivid sight of winged seraphim worshiping and serving God was very real to Isaiah.

When angels made surprising appearances in Scripture, they generally were seen in human form as males. Frequently mistaken for men, as in the case of Abraham, who welcomed "three men," two of whom went to visit Lot in Sodom (Genesis 18:1-8; 19:1), they walked and talked with people. They sat and ate with both Abraham and Lot (Genesis 18:8; 19:3), though it was assumed by most evangelical scholars that the third Person with whom Abraham conversed was the Lord Jehovah, in theophany. When Lot invited his visitors, who appeared to him to be men, to rest and relax, the men of the city lusted to misuse and abuse them sexually (Genesis 19:1-8).

Mark, describing the angel in the tomb of Jesus, describes the man as youthful (Mark 16:5). Luke refers to two men in shining garments (24:4). A single exception to the male gender of angels may be the description of Zechariah, who talked with an angel and two women appeared with wind in their wings (Zechariah 5:9). The meaning of this text, however, is unclear.

It is also a matter of record that angels may appear in any number, from one (Luke 1:26-29) or two (John 20:12; Acts 1:10) to three (Genesis 18:1-2) or four (Revelation 7:1-2; 9:14-15) or many (Luke 2:13).

So unusual and auspicious is the appearance of angels sometimes that the beholder is filled with fear, joy; or wonder, awe, and amazement (Daniel 10:5-6; Matthew 28:3; Luke 24:4; Revelation 4:6-8; 10:1-3; 15:6; 18:1). Sometimes mental or emotional disturbances result from an angel's appearance, as in the case of Zacharias, Mary, and the shepherds (Luke 1:12, 29, 34, 38; 2:9, 15, 18). At other times complete lack of strength or mental exhaustion is effected (Daniel 10:8; Matthew 28:4). It must not be concluded, however, that angels are simply glorified human beings. Matthew states that believers will be like angels in heaven, but he does not quote Jesus as saying they will be angels (22:30). The author of Hebrews distinguishes the innumerable hosts of angels from the spirits of just men made perfect (12:22-23).

### *Angels are beings with time and space limitations, but they have great agility and rapidity of movement*

Although some writers assert that angels are not confined to time or space, or by the changes of either,[54] they do not mean in the absolute sense. Only the infinite is superior to all time and space designations. Angels do change their place, either by sudden and rapid shift of activity from one point to another or because they act at intermediate points. What duration and succession mean to angels we cannot tell. It may be conjectured that angels do not grow old, and the antitheses of youth and old age cannot be applied to them. Yet it must be noted that angels do have a history, for at some point in the past there were angels who rebelled, while others remained loyal to God. We have no record, however, of the development, progress, or advancement of the angels in the sense of continuous history to a state of age or maturity.

On some occasions the Scripture pictures angels as having wings, assuming the seraphim and cherubim are names given to some angel groups. Isaiah's vision of the Lord included a description of seraphim with six wings each. These awesome creatures stood above the throne and covered their faces and their feet and also flew about to perform their duties. Each activity required the use of a pair of wings (Isaiah 6:2, 6).

Cherubim also are described as having wings. Ezekiel's vision portrays them as having four faces and four wings each, with hands under the wings (Ezekiel 1:5-8, 13-14, 24). Their wings provided the speed of motion ascribed to them, while their movement caused the sound like many waters and like an army moving. When they stood, their wings were lowered around them.

On still another occasion Gabriel flew swiftly to Daniel's side (Daniel 9:21). Although not specifically so stating, this reference to flying may imply that Gabriel had wings. John records his vision of an angel "flying in midheaven" (Revelation 14:6-7). We are not informed as to who the angel was. His announcement was of great impending judgment on believers. Thus we cannot conclude that all angels have wings, or that the wings are like birds' wings. Perhaps all that can be said is that wings imply swiftness to do God's will, plus genuine, complete obedience in service, just as wind and fire symbolize quick and fervent service (Hebrews 1:7).

### *Angels are numberless, they do not have connubial relationships, and they are everlasting spirits*

Medieval scholars are said to have argued over how many angels could dance on the head of a pin. Just as inconceivable, if not foolhardy, is the attempt to enumerate the angels. At the birth of Christ there were multitudes of angels (Luke 2:13-15), and these were only part of the heavenly host. The name "The Lord of Hosts" (Psalm 46:7, 11; Isaiah 6:3) may indicate that God has armies of angels. At His betrayal, Christ said He could have had the assistance of twelve legions of angels, perhaps as many as 144,000 (Matthew 26:53). The apostle John saw so many angels in his vision that he used an expression that probably means a number vast beyond comprehension (Revelation 5:11). Hebrews 12:22 states the same thing.

Furthermore, the number of angels must be constant, for Jesus said they do not marry (Matthew 22:28-30), and there is no reason to conclude that angels ever die. Jesus' statement may imply that angels are ungendered, or that they are sexless in the physical sense of reproducing, even if gendered. His words to the Sadducees seem to indicate that angels are immortal and do not die. At least after the resurrection of believers are said to be equal to the angels (Luke 20:34-36). Furthermore, if the devil and his cohorts are tormented day and night forever and ever (Revelation 20:10), it is reasonable to believe that loyal angels will never cease to exist in the bliss of heaven.

## *Angels are not a race*

They were originally moral, free-choosing beings on probation. Those who remained loyal are incorruptible, while the rebellious angels are not redeemable. Closely connected with the previous assertions based on Matthew 22:28-30 and Luke 20:34-36 is the conclusion that angels are more of a "company" than a race.

The human race began with a single pair and the whole race descended from them through natural propagation. They were created male and female, but nothing of this sort is said of the angels. As moral beings the angels were place on probation wit the ability to know right from wrong and choose between them. On this basis the angels, not being part of a race and so not included in some head of the race, must have been loyal or disloyal, obedient or disobedient, individually rather than collectively. It may be as Thiessen suggests, that "because of this fact God has made no provision of salvation for the fallen angels."[55]

When the writer of the Book of Hebrews states that Christ did not give help to the angels but only to the seed of Abraham (Hebrews 2:16), it may be that He found no common nature of angels to take for the redemption He proposed for the human race by joining Himself to humanity and taking the common nature of all.

The moral and probative declarations regarding angels are grounded on the fact that some of them rebelled and fell from an original state of purity and goodness (2 Peter 2:4; Jude 6; Revelation 12:4). Only a statement of fact is needed to assert the pristine character of all the angels created by God originally. The holy character of the Creator determines the carte blanche original holiness of all created "personal," moral beings. Consequently, evil angels are evil only by apostasy.

### *They have limited characteristics*

Angels are described as having certain limited characteristics of personality (without the *imago Dei*, which is reserved for the human family alone), such as intellect, feeling, knowledge, and wisdom. These limited powers are expressed as angels bless and praise the Lord, fulfill His commandments, and obey "the voice of His word," as stated by the psalmist (103:20). There is of necessity an implied intelligence in order for God's claims, His love, and His majesty to be recognized. The response of religious affections in praise and reverence, with voluntary service and worship, undergirds the fact of feeling and intelligence. "With such forms of activity there must be intellect, sensibility, and will — that complex of powers which constitutes personality."[56]

The angel who announced the advent of Christ was quickly joined by the heavenly host that lifted a mighty chorus of joy (Luke 2:9-14). Angels are said to intensely desire to study the mystery of redemption and the sufferings of Christ (1 Peter 1:10-12). Angels also rejoice over one sinner who repents (Luke 15:10). The ministry of angels to Christ after His temptation in the wilderness and during His agonies in Gethsemane portrays their deep sensitivity to pain and suffering.

Although superior to human beings in wisdom and knowledge, angels are not omniscient. An unidentified wise woman of Tekoah commended David for his wisdom in knowing the designs of Joab; she said he had "the wisdom of the angel of God, to know all that is in the earth" (2 Samuel 14:20). It is implied by Christ in Matthew 24:36 that angels have knowledge above that of human beings, but they are not, like God, omniscient. The same limited knowledge is implied by a statement of Peter (1 Peter 1:12), and the authority of the angels is intimated in Paul's charge to Timothy, his son in the gospel (1 Timothy 5:21).

## *Angels excel in strength, they are mighty in power, but they are not omnipotent*

All the powers of the angels, obviously, are derived from God and exercise in obedience to God and at His pleasure alone. The angels cry, "Holy, Holy, Holy, is the Lord God, the Almighty. . . . Thou didst create all things, and because of Thy will they existed, and were created" (Revelation 4:8, 11). God sent two angels to destroy the wicked city of Sodom, but by their power they also spared Lot from judgment (Genesis 19:12-16). When David sinned in numbering Israel and Judah, an angel was sent to smite Jerusalem with a pestilence (2 Samuel 24:14-17). In the Book of Revelation when powerful judgments are meted out through the angels, Christ is pictured as being in full control (Revelation 6:16, passim).

Just as angelic power is wielded in judgment, so God also shows reserve and mercy through His angels. The angel could have, and probably would have, destroyed Jerusalem after David's sin, had it not been for the mercy of God (2 Samuel 24:13-16). Also, in Revelation 7:1-3, angelic messengers are restrained until God has worked to protect His own servants by the seal on their foreheads. Even Satan's powerful forces are held back by God's holy angels and are then defeated (Revelation 12:7-9).

When David wrote that angels excel in strength, the clear implication is that their strength is superior to that of humans (Psalm 103:20). Peter states that angels are greater in power and might than false teachers, who insult or speak evil of dignities, yet they also do not accuse them before God (2 Peter 2:10-11). Angels will exercise their power in gathering believers at Christ's return to earth (Matthew 24:30-31). An angel released Peter from a locked prison where he was bound with chains (Acts 12:7-11). Great strength was needed to roll a huge stone, which may have weighed as much as four tons, from the tomb of Christ (Matthew 28:2; Mark 16:3-4). A final reference to the power and strength of the angels is given by Paul, when he wrote comforting words to the believers at Thessalonica, who were in the throes of persecution, telling them that they would be avenged and the wicked would be punished (2 Thessalonians 1:7-10).

### *The angels are distinguished by the use of various names that may imply orders, ranks, or classifications*

All the angels fall into one of two general categories — the good angels and the evil angels. Most interpreters of Scripture see at least four or more subdivisions of the good angels. Pseudo-Dionysus's categories of nine separate choirs may largely be disregarded for our consideration of any biblical hierarchy.[57]

It is unthinkable that anything under the headship of Christ would be disorganized or disorderly. Thus when the angels are mentioned in group context as the Lord's hosts or armies, as is frequently done in Scripture (*e.g.*, 2 Kings 6:16-17; Psalms 68:12, 14, 17; 103:20-21; 148:2), there is every reason to assume that angels are organized into grades and ranks, as in any military operation that calls for the highest order. But since the Bible is so indefinite as to what this organization may be, we can only conjecture what real hierarchy exists.

Graham and many others cite Colossians 1:16 as a reference to angelic or celestial beings, so that thrones, dominions, principalities, and powers become designations of grades of angels with varied spheres of operation and levels of authority implied. Graham concludes that the order may well be as follows: archangels, angels, seraphim, cherubim, principalities, authorities, powers, thrones, might, and dominion.[58] Wesley gives no comment on Colossians 1:16 in his *Notes Upon the New Testament*, but other authorities question whether Paul refers to celestial beings in this passage.

Michael alone is singled out in the Bible as an archangel (Jude 9). There is no plural form for archangel used in Scripture. The prefix *arch-* suggests that Michael is the chief or principal angel above all angels. Even his name means he is "like unto the Lord." Michael is associated with Israel in the Old Testament and in the Book of Daniel he is shown to be the prince who stands as a protective ally to God's people (Daniel 10:21; 12:1). At the end of the age Michael is locked in deadly combat against Satan and all his forces, with the clear prediction of total victory (Revelation 12:7-12). Some Bible scholars believe that it was Michael who expelled Lucifer, perhaps an archangel also before his fall, out of heaven. Paul states that it will be the voice of the archangel that will announce the second coming of Christ (1 Thessalonians 4:16).

Some authorities think that Gabriel qualifies as an archangel, but he is never so designated.[59] Mentioned by name only four times in the Bible, Gabriel always bears good news (Daniel 8:16; 9:21; Luke 1:19, 26). He seems to be God's foremost messenger of mercy and hope. Even his name means "God's hero" or "the mighty one of God." It seems clear that wherever Gabriel appears in the Bible he is the special messenger of God to communicate a divine revelation and interpretation concerning God's plan and program for his people Israel and His Messiah.

Two special classifications of angelic beings in Scripture need to be explained. They are the cherubim and the seraphim, already noted in various connections. The cherubim are the first to be mentioned. They are the spiritual beings equipped with flaming swords to prevent access to the tree of life to Adam and Eve after they were expelled from the Garden of Eden (Genesis 3:24). From this it is evident that sin and the tree of life, a symbol of immortality, are not compatible.

Cherubim next appear as figures on either end of the Ark of the Covenant in the Holy of Holies of the tabernacle. Between and beneath their outstretched wings, a combined span of fifteen feet, was the mercy seat, which covered the Ark. Thus mentioned in Exodus 25:10-22, they are associated with the localized presence of God among His people. Depictions of the cherubim are woven into the design of the veil of the tabernacle, as well as its inner curtain (Exodus 26, 36; the actual construction of these fabrics is reported in Exodus 37: 1-9). Again, in Numbers 7:89 the cherubim are mentioned. God's presence is said to be between them as He spoke to Moses. Further mention is made of the cherubim when the temple of Solomon was constructed (1 Kings 6:14-18; 8:2-11; 2 Kings 19:15; 2 Chronicles 3:5-14; 5:7-14).

After the temple was destroyed, Ezekiel included the cherubim in visionary description. Although not mentioned in the first chapter, the four living creatures are identified as cherubim later (Ezekiel 10:1-22: 28:13-19). Even when the ark of the covenant was gone, the cherubim were still represented (Ezekiel 41:15-26).

The primary service of the cherubim seems to be to uphold the glory of God. They are never termed angels, perhaps because they are not messengers in the sense of carrying messages from God to human persons. They seem rather to proclaim and protect "God's glorious presence, His sovereignty, and His holiness,"[60] thus bringing judgment against those who fail to honor Him. Of the ninety-two times cherubim are mentioned in the Bible, either in the singular or in the plural, only one reference is made in the New Testament. In Hebrews 9:5 the cherubim of glory are shown in the description of the shekinah glory of God's presence. Some scholars believe the references to "living creatures" in the Apocalypse are to the cherubim.

A final series of interesting references to the cherubim or allusions to them in the Psalms should be noted. In Psalm 18:9-10, the cherubim are shown in theophanic depictions of some type in which God's movements are shown to people at cloud level. There may be a possible connection between the Hebrew words *kerub* ("cherub") and *rechub* ("chariot"), with further allusions possible in Psalms 80:1; 99:1; 104:1-4.

The seraphim are distinct from the cherubim, and their duties seem to be different. Whereas the cherubim are protectors of God's glory and proclaimers of His grace that provides salvation, the seraphim seem to perform a priestly type of service for God. The all-consuming devotion of the seraphim is depicted by their name, which means "burning ones." They are shown hovering over the throne on which the Lord sits, in the only place they are mentioned in Scripture (Isaiah 6). The cherubim, on the other hand, are below the throne.

If clouds are symbolic of the cherubim enveloping and conveying God as in a chariot, then the symbol of the seraphim may possibly be the burning coals of fire that were taken from the altar and touched the lips of Isaiah. Thus purified, his lips were inspired to speak for God, just as the seraphim lifted praise to the holy Trinity in the trisagion.

### *The work or ministry of angels for God in behalf of the heirs of salvation is varied and diverse*

A. Angels desire to look into the mystery of redemption, but they must remain observers, not partakers, of the revelation of redeeming love, of the mystery of the Incarnation and the plan of redemption (Ephesians 3:10; 1 Peter 1:12).

B. Angels are under the headship of Christ and unite in harmony and fellowship, as messengers of God, to redeem the fallen human race (Colossians 1:20; 1 Peter 3:22).

C. Angels minister to those who are the heirs of salvation (Hebrews 1:13-14).

D. While Christ is the only Mediator between God and man (1 Timothy 2:5), angels were messengers of God to Christ (John 1:51; Hebrews 1:7), a fact that does not imply the metaphysical idea of the Gnostics.

E. Christ will send His angels to gather the elect for the day of judgment (Matthew 24:21).

F. The angels who remain loyal to God are ever pure, holy, and good, giving continual obedient service (Psalm 103:20-21; Matthew 6:10; Revelation 4:8-11).

G. The concept of guardian angels is probably a fanciful interpretation of Matthew 18:10 or Acts 12:15, as is the concept of presiding angels of various nations (Daniel 10:13).

H. Angels were associated with the giving of the law in Jewish tradition (Acts 7:53; Galatians 3:19; Hebrews 2:2).

I. Angels are not to be worshiped (Colossians 2:18; Hebrews 2:7; 2 Peter 2:11; Revelation 19:10).

J. The natural, permanent abode of angels is in heaven (Matthew 22:30; Luke 2:13, 15; John 1:51).

K. Angels ministered to Christ in His temptation and His sufferings (Matthew 4:11; Luke 22:43), they announced His resurrection and ascension (Matthew 28:2; Acts 1:10-11), they bear the spirits of believers to Abraham's bosom (Luke 16:22), and they are to attend Christ at His second coming and gather His people into the kingdom (Matthew 12:39; 16:27; 24:31).

L. Angels keep those who abide in the secret place of the Most High and protect His servants from their enemies (2 Kings 6:15-17; Psalms 91:1, 11-12; Daniel 6:22; Acts 5:19; 12:8, 11).

M. Angels cheer God's servants and reveal His purpose to them (Matthew 1:20; 2:13, 19-20; Luke 1:11-13, 19; Acts 8:26; 10:3-6; 27:23-24).

N. Angles execute judgment on God's enemies and officiate at the judgment of nations (2 Kings 19:35; Matthew 13:30, 39, 40-50; Acts 12:23; 2 Thessalonians 1:7-8).

O. The messengers of God do not act on their own initiative but as directly commissioned by God, thus they are completely God-centered in their work and worship (Luke 1:19; Hebrews 1:14; Revelation 4-5).

P. Angels interpret God's will to men (Daniel 7:16; 10:5, 11; Zechariah 1:9, 13-14, 19; 2:3; 4:1, 4-5; 5:5, 10; 6:4-5).

Volumes have been written with speculative indiscretion concerning angels, both good and evil. Although imaginative discourse may be interesting and intriguing, we may best be satisfied by adhering closely to the Scriptures. Struggles with biblical interpretation may never end; interpretations may be less than satisfactory, but the Bible remains the only reliable source of information concerning angels.

# PART II

## Demonology

*Say first — for Heaven hides nothing from thy view,*
*Nor the deep tract of Hell — say first what cause*
*Moved our grand Parents, in that happy state,*
*Favored of Heaven so highly to fall off*
*From their Creator, and transgress his will*
*For one restraint, lords of the World derides.*
*The infernal Serpent; he it was whose guile,*
*Stirred up with envy and revenge, deceived*
*The other of mankind, what time his pride*
*Had cast him out of Heaven, with all his host*
*Of rebel Angels, by whose aid, aspiring*
*To set himself in glory above his peers,*
*He trusted to have equaled the Most High,*
*If he opposed, and, with ambitious aim*
*Against the throne and monarchy of God,*
*Raised impious war in Heaven and battle proud,*
*With vain attempt.*[61]

THE "PERSONAL LIKE," REAL existence of a spirit of evil is clearly revealed in the Bible. Likewise, belief in the existence of evil spirits has prevailed among all the known peoples of the world from the earliest times of which there is any knowledge at all. This follows naturally upon the belief in the survival of the human spirit, for among primitive and savage people, evil as well as good persons are believed to survive after death. But the belief is also based on the revelation that was made in a progressive manner by the Lord Himself to His chosen people, Israel, and through His Son Jesus Christ to Jews and Gentiles alike. There is evidence to show that evil spirits are malignant and hostile to the living, for a variety of reasons, and that they are led by a chief of unusual power and malignancy.

# 9

## *Demons: Definition and Delineation*

THE HISTORY OF VARIOUS religions from the earliest times shows a universal belief in demons led by a powerful head. In archaeological discoveries from Babylon and Sumeria various forms of demonological phenomena are abundant. The antiquities of Egypt, Assyria, Chaldea, Greece, and Rome are laced with demonic phenomena, including spells, incantations, magical texts, and exorcisms. Merrill F. Unger states that to an amazing degree, "the history of religion is an account of demon-controlled religion, particularly in its clash with the Hebrew faith and later with Christianity."[62]

Among certain peoples of other cultures there remains a strong belief in evil spirits besides departed human spirits. Since some of these spirits betray strong animal characteristics, these people assume that many demons are the surviving spirits of animals, particularly of such creatures as are generally feared by man; for example, snakes and other reptiles, four-footed jungle animals, and poisonous biting creatures. At the time when these demonic beliefs had their rise, there seems to have been a very intimate relation between the animal and the human world. Consequently, there was no difficulty in believing that people might be attacked and possessed by the spirits of animals. Such beliefs were well attested during the Middle Ages and remain in many parts of the world today.[63]

Belief in demons at times has the appearance of being simply the result of a creative imagination. It is easy to imagine the existence of shapes and forms other than those that can be seen with the natural eyes and to endow them with human or animal characteristics. Other demons are clearly the result of personification. Such maladies as a common headache, a fever, and the plague may be personified as demons. Certain moral qualities such as evil thoughts, lust, and falsehood have also been so personified.

The fact that similar demonological conceptions are found among so many different and widely separated people may be accounted for by the common reaction of the human mind, by the hypothesis of borrowing, or by the theory of a common primitive revelation. Some demonic conceptions, or course, may be the product of the religious genius of particular people. The belief in the continued existence of both good and evil departed human spirits is fundamental to the Jewish and Christian faith. This is also the prevailing belief among practically all the people of the world, and it can be stated with certainty that nearly all, if not all, have believed in the survival of the soul after death, at least temporarily.[64]

The belief in demons and in Satan, or the devil, as shown in the New Testament, was common to the Jews and their pagan neighbors at the time of Christ, and the New Testament leaves no question that Satan is the head of the whole kingdom of evil. A study of the biblical names and references to Satan and his cohorts will be followed by a general summary of the nature, character, work, and destiny of Satan. The final section of this study will be devoted to the development of a doctrine of demonology.

# 10

## *Demons: Scriptural Names, Terms, and References*

ONE OF THE MOST interesting features of the doctrine of Satan in the Old Testament, as with all biblical truth, is that it is progressively revealed. The gradual development of this doctrine may be seen to some extent through the use of the Hebrew word *satan*.

The word *satan* is first used generally in the realm of human relationships, then in the conflict between the human and spirit worlds. There is a marked transition from a verb to an appellation and finally to a proper name. Although it would be helpful to know for certain the chronological order of the Old Testament books, this is not imperative for understanding the facts that are known about Satan in the Old Testament.[65]

The Hebrew word means *to lie in wait, to oppose*, or *to be an adversary*.[66] A. C. Knudson states that the word had the general meaning of adversary and that it was used exclusively in that sense in the earlier literature of the Old Testament. An example of this usage is found in Numbers 22:22-35 in the story of Balaam, whose dumb beast rebuked him for beating it. "But God was angry . . .and the angel of the Lord took his stand in the way as an adversary against him" (v. 22). In verse 32 the same word is used: "Behold, I have come out as an adversary, because your way is contrary to me." Here the angel of the Lord speaks and the meaning of *satan* is clearly that of adversary.

A. B. Davidson states that the word *satan* means *one who opposes another in his purpose or pretension and claims*. The following Scriptures show this meaning:[68]

- But the commanders of the Philistines were angry with him, and the commanders of the Philistines said to him, "Make the man go back, that he may return to his place where you have assigned him, and do not let him go down to battle with us, lest in battle he become an adversary to us" (1 Samuel 29:4).

- David then said, "What have I to do with you, O sons of Zeruiah, that you should this day be an adversary to me?" (2 Samuel 19:22).

- But now the Lord my God has given me rest on every side; there is neither adversary nor misfortune (1 Kings 5:4).

- Then the Lord raised up an adversary to Solomon, Hadad the Edomite; he was of the royal line in Edom (1 Kings 11:14).

- God also raised up another adversary to him, Rezon the son of Eliada, who had fled from his lord Hadadezer king of Zobah (1 Kings 11:23).

- So he was an adversary to Israel all the days of Solomon, along with the evil that Hadad did; and he abhorred Israel and reigned over Syria (1 Kings 11:25).

*Satan* appears further in the Old Testament as the name of a specific angel, "the opposer," whose task is to oppose people in their profession of a right standing and relationship with God, as well as to test their sincerity. This is seen in the Book of Job where "the *satan*" questions the truth and sincerity of Job. The opposer or adversary is seen again in the Book of Zechariah, where he is ready to remind God in an unfriendly spirit of the sins of Joshua the high priest (Zechariah 3:1). In Chronicles the opposer prompts David to do an act that will bring him into disfavor with God. "Satan stood up against Israel, and incited David to number Israel" (1 Chronicles 21:1 RSV). This seems to be a parallel passage with 2 Samuel 24:1, where "the anger of the Lord" is said to have incited David to number Israel.

The Hebrew word *satan* is used only thirty-one times in the Old Testament, according to Robert Young.[69] In the King James Version the word is not translated in seventeen instances,[70] where it is simply transliterated "satan." Except in 1 Chronicles 22:1, cited above, *satan* does not appear as a true proper name. In all other uses the word has the article, which distinctly sets it forth to mean "the opposer." Thus it is translated twelve times in the King James Version as "adversary" (Numbers 22:22; 1 Samuel 29:4; 2 Samuel 19:22; 1 Kings 5:4; 11:4, 23, 25, Psalms 38:20; 71:13; 109:4; 20, 29), with the remaining two times being translated "resist" in Zechariah 3:1 and "to withstand" in Numbers 22:22. In Psalms 38:20 and 109:4, the word is used as a verb and its meaning is "to be" or "to act as" an opposer.

The Hebrew word is used twice in reference to the angel of the Lord who stood in the way of Balaam's donkey, and several times it is used of men in their relationships with one another. For example, men are referred to as being adversaries or satans to others. Thus Hadad and Rezon were adversaries of Israel (1 Kings 5:14, 23, 25). The sons of Zeruiah were adversaries of David, and David himself was referred to as a satan by the Philistine princes who chided Achish for including David in their forces lest he become a traitor during the battle that ensued (1 Samuel 29:4).

The term may also refer to an accuser before the judgment seat as in Psalm 109:6-7:

*Appoint a wicked man over him;*
*And let an accuser stand at his right hand.*
*When he is judged, let him come forth guilty;*
*And let his prayer become sin.*

In verse 20 the adversaries are said to be from the Lord and in verse 4 the wicked and deceitful are the writer's accusers.

In the Book of Job and in Zechariah the word *satan* is used as a noun or an appellation and is preceded by the definite article, giving constant repetition of the term *the satan*. A study of the word *satan* shows clearly that it is used in reference to human relationships as describing (1) an enemy, (2) one who opposes another, and (3) an unjust accusation. As a verbal noun *satan* is used to describe the conflict between the human and the spirit world, such as in the conflict between Balaam and the angel of the Lord, then as an appellation in the Books of Job and Zechariah, and, finally, as a proper name in 1 Chronicles, the last becoming a fixed usage in the New Testament.[71]

# 11

## *The Devil — Satan*

WE NEED NOT RESORT to speculation when it comes to the identification of the Devil or Satan, or with respect to the names by which he is known in Scripture. The Apocalypse of John brings all the names together, although this is not to suggest that he was so identified and understood throughout biblical history. We have seen that there has been, as with most other topics of biblical theology, a progression of thought and a development of understanding of the person and work of Satan. John's record is unimpeachable on this subject:

> And there was war in heaven, Michael and his angels waging war with the dragon. And the dragon and his angels waged war, and they were not strong enough, and there was no longer a place found for them in heaven. And the great dragon was thrown down, the serpent of old who is called the devil and Satan, who deceives the world [margin reads "inhabited earth"]; he was thrown down to the earth, and his angels were thrown down with him (Revelation 12:7-9).[72]

John Wesley does not identify the time when Satan was cast down to earth, but he writes, "So till now he had a place in heaven." He then compares this with Luke 10:18 and Ephesians 2:2; 4:8; 6:12. Continuing, Wesley states:

> He is termed the great dragon, as appearing here in that shape, to intimate his poisonous and cruel disposition. The ancient serpent — In allusion to his deceiving Eve in that form. . . He has deceived the whole world — Not only in their first parents, but through all ages, and in all countries, into unbelief and all wickedness; into the hating and persecuting faith and all goodness. He was cast out unto the earth — He was cast out of heaven; and being cast out thence, himself came to the earth. Nor had he been unemployed on the earth before, although his ordinary abode was in heaven.[73]

## *The original nature, state, and character of Satan*

Probably at no point in theology has there been a greater misuse or abuse of the imagination than in the speculation surrounding Satan — his origin, character, and existence. The human imagination seems always more fertile when dealing with evil than when dealing with good. Perhaps this is so because evil is less evil in imagination than in reality, whereas good is always better in reality than in imagination.

From ancient rabbinic tradition the speculation grows that Satan was created the sixth day at the same time as Eve, that he was the highest throne-angel and had twelve wings (twice the number specified for the seraphim of Isaiah 6 and of the living creatures of Ezekiel 1 and Revelation 4) and that he led other angels who, like him, were envious of Adam for having had the privilege of naming all the creatures God had made. A camel-like creature with arms and legs, hands and feet, called a serpent, was then selected to deceive Eve and tempt her to sin. As one might suspect, apocryphal and apocalyptic literature is even more vividly imaginary. In the Middle Ages people came to picture the devil as a huge black cat. Later he was pictured as a goat and finally as a horned, tailed, hoofed, and hairy Satan with bat ears, wings, and a pitchfork. Some of these images are still "popular" and continue in the minds of people.

The true picture and concept of Satan can be derived only from the Judeo-Christian Scriptures, which are not very explicit at many points. Even so, contemporary Christians are not at all committed to all of the crude imagery that has accrued around a belief in Satan. Various reasons have been given as to why there is so little material and detail concerning Satan in the Old Testament. One valid reason, according to John P. Newport, may have been the determination of God to lead His people to a dynamic, practical monotheism. In the midst of the pagan, polytheistic ancient world, the primary emphasis of God's revelation was placed on the supremacy and power of the Holy One of Abraham, Isaac, and Jacob.[74] Newport continues with the following statement:

> Despite the controversy over such Old Testament passages as Genesis 3:1-19, Isaiah 14:12-15, and Ezekiel 28:12 the Bible suggests that from the early moments of the creation of this world Satan was on the scene, a rebel against God. Pride seems to have been the cause of his fall. Following the suggestion in Revelation 12:9, it is said that Satan became disguised as a serpent. He is seen as the agent of temptation for the first man and woman (Genesis 3:10; 20:2). Although there is not much in the Old Testament about Satan, when he does appear he is always the adversary of God's people. He seeks to lead God's people into presumption (1 Chronicles 21:1) or slanders them to God's face (Zechariah 3:1).[75]

Echoing the traditional view, which is based on the solid premise of faith in God as the ultimate, eternal, personal Being, of unlimited wisdom, power, and goodness, there is no adequate reason why we may not assume that Satan was created as an angel of the highest rank. Subsequently he lost his purity, holiness, and goodness through an act of rebellion, most likely because of envy or pride arising out of distrust (John 16:7-11), whereupon he enlisted numerous angels as allies, perhaps as many as one-third of all those whom God had created. Because Satan and his cohorts revolted and fell, they were cast out of heaven. Given a limited degree of freedom on earth, Satan and his angels are now engaged in false accusations, because Satan "is a liar and the father of lies";

in deceptions, because Satan is the deceiver, and in the destruction of believers, because Satan is a murderer from the very beginning of his revolt.

> While the fall of the angels is clearly stated (Jude 6) and also their eventual fate (Matthew 25:41), the rest of the traditional explanation rests upon the tenuous foundation of a highly symbolic passage (Revelation 12:3-4, 7-9) and the reading in of a deeper meaning into two poetic denunciations of the kings of Babylon and Tyre (Isaiah 14:12-14; Ezekiel 28:12-17) . . . the theory seems to be the best that can be offered on the meager basis available for interpretation. It is in accord with what we know about the nature of God, the nature of evil, and the activities of Satan.[76]

## *The fall, moral character, and personality of Satan*

It is unthinkable that the God of the Old and New Testament Scriptures, pictured as holy and wise, pure and good, would create anything at all in any other way than after His own plan and will, ex nihilo. To begin with God plus nothing is a radical monotheism, as noted by Dennis F. Kinlaw: "There is one ultimate because there is one *primus* and that is Yahweh. There is no world either good or evil that exists alongside Him as equal or rival." One must then conclude, as does Kinlaw, that evil is transferred from the metaphysical to the moral realm.[77]

There is no room in the understanding of God's Person, nature, and being for a cosmic dualism. God reigns, and He reigns alone, ultimately. Satan exists and is real. There is conflict of a cosmic nature between God and Satan, but it is temporary, limited, and bounded by God's complete control. And in spite of the existence of Satan, the human family stands totally responsible for sin and its consequences. The freedom of Satan, of the angels, of Adam and Eve, and of all moral beings is all that is needed to account for sin and evil with their consequences.

> No cosmic evil principle exists that makes sin necessary. Satan may entice man to sin, but he is finite like the mortal creature he tempts and is subject to the same righteous judgment of Yahweh. The serpent could only encourage Eve to misuse her freedom as he had misused his.[78]

One need not linger over the account of the serpent in the Garden of Eden, but it is intriguing to note that Adam Clarke concluded that the creature that Satan used to deceive Eve was not a snake of reptile variety, as the English word connotes. It was rather a type of ape, most likely the orangutan (meaning man of the forest), whose characteristics, Clarke claims, are much more in harmony with the description provided by the Genesis account.[79] The most we can conclude is that "the account of the probation and fall of man found in Genesis 3:1-24 is an inspired record of historical fact bound up with a deep and rich symbolism."[80]

We can only deduce from the immoral character of Satan and the fallen angels as presently revealed in Scripture that they were created free spirit beings. The term *moral* means the power of choice between good and evil, attended by understanding, the capacity of contrary choice, and various alternatives present from which to choose. Satan, now being totally corrupted and beyond recovery, has only the power of contrariness, hence he is the adversary who always opposes God, man, and the good.

Satan's person is not that of human personhood. He is a person only in the broadest sense of being a real spiritual being. He is thus described, among numerous designations, as "the ruler of this world" (John 12:31; 14:30; 16:11), "the prince of the power of the air" (Ephesians 2:20, "the good of this world" (2 Corinthians 4:4), "the ruler of the demons" (Matthew 12:24; Luke 11:15), "the evil one" (John 17:15; 1 John 2:13, 14; 5:18, 29), "the tempter" (Matthew 4:3; 1 Thessalonians 3:5), "the accuser" (Revelation 12:10), and "deceiver" (Revelation 12:9; 20:3).

## *The position, power, and destiny of Satan*

Many of the foregoing descriptive terms applied to Satan in the Bible suggest various dimensions of his position and power. But more than these are the suggestions that Satan does have a dominion, a kingdom with subjects, and a certain royal dignity. Jude 9 indicates that even Michael, one of the highest of God's messengers, respected the devil and called upon the Lord Himself to rebuke him.

To hold the doctrine of Satan and to credit him with limited power does not mean that God is less than omnipotent. The Devil at his best or at his worst never is able to do more than to counterfeit God's truth (Ephesians 2:2; 2 Corinthians 11:13-15; 2 Thessalonians 2:8-11; 1 Timothy 4:1-3), or to counterfeit God's rule, as noted above. His sole purpose is that of perversion — to impose disorder and chaos on order and design in the cosmos.[81] Wittaker Chambers may have best characterized Satan when he imagined a conversation between himself and the Devil. Satan admitted shamelessly that he had the will to be creative, thus he was full of pride; but he was incapable of creating anything, therefore he was sterile and full of envy.[82] Perhaps it is true of those who have a form of godliness but do not have its power — a woeful situation that will prevail in the "last days" (2 Timothy 3:1-5) — that they, like Satan, being devoid of both love and goodness, can never create anything of lasting value.

Even though there is no clear evidence of when Satan was created as a holy angel or when he fell, there is no doubt as to his final destination. The precise times of his defeat, his being bound in the bottomless pit, and his being cast into the lake of fire that burns forever and ever are not known. But since it is clearly stated that his doom will be at the end of the age, it is one of the most certain facts of biblical revelation. Writing in highly figurative language, John leaves no uncertainty in the Apocalypse as to Satan's end (Revelation 20:1-10).

# 12

## *The Relationship of Fallen Angels to Demons and Evil Spirits*

MUCH OF WHAT HAS been stated above concerning Satan and the fallen angels, with their activity and characteristics, is also relevant to demons and evil spirits as portrayed in Scripture. J. Stafford Wright gives some attention to two groups of fallen spirits and avers that there were two falls of spiritual beings, one at the time Satan fell, prior to the fall of Adam, the other fall occurring subsequent to the fall of Adam, involving the sons of God (angels) and the daughters of men (Genesis 6:2).

Wright also links the difficult passages of Isaiah 14 and Ezekiel 28 to the description of Satan's fall.[83] There is evidence in 2 Peter 2:4 and Jude 6-7 that there are two groups of fallen angels, some reserved in "eternal bonds" for "judgment" in *Tartarus*, and others free at present to consort with Satan against God and man, but there is little evidence for two falls. Some authorities reject the imagery of "sons of God" or the "morning stars" of Genesis 6:2; Job 1:6; 2:1; 38:7, as referring at all to the angels, fallen or unfallen.[84] In his *Explanatory Notes Upon the Old Testament*, John Wesley sees all the references in Job listed above as being angels, but interprets the Genesis account of "sons of God" (6:2), as the righteous descendants of Seth who intermarried with those of Cain, the murderer.[85]

The identification of demons with fallen angels has been made by numerous authorities, and it has become the traditional view,[86] based on such Scriptures as Daniel 10:13, 20 and Revelation 12:7, 9. Thiessen says that this view has the "advantage of simplicity and obviates the necessity of inquiring any further as to the origin of demons."[87] He raises two problems with the theory: (1) there is no indication that a fallen angel ever is described in Scripture as seeking embodiment in a human person and (2) it seems incongruous to state that a person has been possessed by a fallen angel, though such possession would be possible if demons and fallen angels are identical.[88]

Other explanations for the identity of demons are unquestionably less tenable. Many of the early Christian writers, along with Philo and Josephus, thought demons were the spirits of deceased wicked men. Contemporary Judaism agrees essentially with the superstitious demonology of Josephus, who stated that demons were the "spirits of the wicked that enter into men that are alive."[89] The obvious conclusion to this theory is that the numbers of demons would constantly increase, showing themselves with increasing frequency as a Stalin or a Hitler. Concerning this view we must agree with the following:

> We object that the Scriptures everywhere represent the unsaved dead as in Sheol and Hades, and not as roaming around on earth (Psalms 9:17; Ezekiel 32:17-24; Luke 16:23; Revelation 20:13). Besides, our Lord has the keys of Hades and is not likely to allow these wicked souls to get out and roam around on the earth (Revelation 1:18).[90]

Another view with alleged scriptural support is that demons are disembodied spirits of a race that inhabited the earth prior to Adam. These spirits are distinguished from angels in that the latter are not mere disembodied spirits but were spiritual beings from the moment of their creation. New Testament support is cited for the distinction between angels and demons (*e.g.*, Luke 8:32; 20:36; 24:39; Acts 23:8-9; 2 Corinthians 5:2-3; Philemon 3:21). The angel

Gabriel and the princes of Persia and Grecia are likewise distinguished from demons in the Old Testament, the latter being identified with the "familiar spirits," the *shedhim*, translated *demons* in the NASB (Deuteronomy 32:17, *goat demon*; Isaiah 13:21, *shaggy goat*; and Isaiah 34:14, *hairy goat*); the *seirim*, translated in the LXX as *daimonia*, hence, the connection with the goat-demon-satyrs; and the *lilith* are considered identical to the demons.[91]

A final view already alluded to is that demons are the result of angels cohabiting with antediluvian women, as based on the LXX and manuscripts of the Codex Alexandrinus, which vary between the translation in Genesis 6:2 "sons of God" and "angels of God." Opposing this "angel theory" have been such notables as Chrysostom, Cyril of Alexandria, and Theodoret and many later theologians including Keil, Lange, Jamieson, Faussett, Brown, Hengstenberg, Matthew Henry, and C. I. Scofield.[92]

Chapter 15 of the Book of Enoch is the most likely basis for this view. It includes the following:

> Wicked spirits came out of the body of them [the daughters of men], for they were generated out of human beings, and from the watchers [angels] flows the beginning of their creation and their primal foundation. The spirits of heaven — in the earth is their dwelling, and the spirits begotten upon earth — in the earth shall be their dwelling. And the spirits of the giants will devour, oppress, destroy, assault, do battle, and cast upon the earth and cause convulsions.

The same projection is made by Philo, Josephus, many rabbinical writers, and the oldest church fathers, such as Justin, Cyprian, Tertullian, Ambrose, and Lactantius. Martin Luther also accepted the idea, as have many more recent scholars, including Koppen, Twesten, Dreschler, Hofmann, Baumgarten, Delitzsch, A. C. Gaebelein, and William Kelly.[93]

Although all of the theories reviewed are beset with various problems that cannot be resolved by present data to the satisfaction of everyone, we must reject the view that identifies "sons of God" in Genesis 6:2 and Job 1:6; 2:1 with celestial beings, on the basis of the arguments of Keil, cited above.[94] The identification of fallen angels with demons and evil spirits, especially as described in the New Testament, is more in keeping with the general tenor of Scripture than other views. Unger states it poignantly as follows:

> The consideration of practical moment, however, as Scriptural reserve reveals, is not whence the demons came, but that they actually are, that they are evil and harmful spirit personalities, that in their fellowship there is no safety, and that against them continual warfare must be waged.[95]

# 13

## *Demon Worship and Demon Possession*

THE VIEW THAT SOME have taken that biblical references to demons and demon possession signify only personifications of incurable diseases scarcely needs mention. T. Witton Davies calls demon possession nothing more than "certain diseases superstitiously regarded as due to demonical influence."[96] But Scripture vividly presents the subject of demonism in such true-to-life portraits that one is ready to conclude, as does Luther Lee, that those who deny the existence of demons and their influence also deny most other Bible doctrines.

> When Christ has been divested of all divine attributes, and reduced to the level of a very good man; when the miracles He wrought have been explained away, when the direct influence of the Holy Spirit is denied, and regeneration is made to consist of the habits of life; and when all future punishment is denied, and hell is converted into the grave, or is made to exist only in the human mind, composed of the elements of a guilty conscience, then there is little room left in the system, for the existence and influence of demons or evil spirits, and they are easily reduced to the fleshly element in every man to some bodily disease, or to some personal human adversary, as the exegesis of different texts may require. The question of the existence of demons is so intimately connected with the various parts of the Christian system, as to render it a matter of considerable importance.[97]

In the New Testament text of Westcott and Hort, the term *daimon* is used only in Matthew 8:31. The Textus Receptus has the word in four other places (Mark 5:12; Luke 8:29; Revelation 16:14; 18:2). The noun *daimonion* occurs sixty-three times, and the verb *daimonizomai* is used thirteen times in the New Testament, while *daimoniōdēs* appears only in James 3:15, and in each case these words should be translated consistently as demon(s), demon possessed, or demonic.

Since there is only one devil, strictly considered, any form of the word should be avoided for the translation of these Greek terms. Everywhere else in the New Testament, demons are designated as *pneumata* ("spirits"). The interchange of *daimon* and *pneuma* supports the identification of demons and spirits in Luke 10:17-20 (cf. Also Matthew 8:16; 10:1, 8). The precise and invariable meaning of these terms in the New Testament is thus seen to be that of evil spirit or messenger/minister of the Devil.[98]

As spiritual beings, demons are unclean; they are vicious, intelligent, and able to attack human persons with moral and spiritual pollution as well as with physical harm and abuse. Throughout the Gospels (Matthew 8:16; 17:18; Mark 9:25; Luke 10:17, 20) demons are shown to be spiritual beings. In some cases — *e.g.*, the Gadarene demoniac (Mark 5:2-16; Luke 8:27-38) and Mary Magdalene, out of whom Jesus cast seven demons (Mark 16:9; Luke 8:2) — numerous demons may possess one person. The apostles Paul and John likewise lend support to the spiritual nature of demons in such passages as Ephesians 2:2, 6:12; and Revelation 16:14, among others.

Furthermore, demons in their possession of human beings are unclean (Mark 3:11-12; Luke 4:36); they are violent and malicious (Matthew 8:28); they are agents or emissaries of Satan (Matthew 12:26-27; 25:41); they afflict the human body with various physical maladies (Matthew 4:24; 12:22: 17:15-18); they obstruct the truth and lead people into personal corruption (1 Timothy 4:1-3; 2 Peter 2:10-12); and they strive to prevent believers from living clean, spiritual lives (Ephesians 6:12; 1 Timothy 4:1).

At no other time in recorded biblical history were the demons more active than during the live of Christ. The unusual fury that was unleashed by Satan seems to indicate his intent to oppose and crush the Messiah. This animosity was predicted as early as Genesis 3:15. The synoptic Gospels describe numerous cases of demon possession, all of which were followed by expulsion of the demons. Christ not only cast out demons everywhere He met them but He also gave this power to His disciples (Mark 3:15; Luke 10:17). That the disciples (believers/apostles) exercised this power also is well illustrated in the Book of Acts (5:16; 8:7; 16:16-18; 19: 12-19). Although in the epistles there are no direct references to demoniacs or the expulsion of demons, there may be allusions in such passages as 1 Corinthians 10:20; 12:10; and 1 Timothy 4:1-2. Apocalyptic demonology clearly implies strong demonic influence and possession (Revelation 9:1-11, 20-21; 16:13-16).

It is noteworthy that the incidence of demon possession was nearly as widespread during the early church ages as in the time of Christ. The Shepherd of Hermas and the Epistle of Barnabas (*ca.* 110-130) show significant content relating to demon possession, and both Justin Martyr and Tertullian were acquainted with the casting out of demons. The same holds true for almost every age of church history, until at present there are so many documentations of possession and deliverance from demons from all sections of the church world that one can scarcely be certain how much of even the top of the iceberg is known and seen. The last hundred years have probably produced more documented cases of demon possessions and expulsions than any previous time in church history. Since World War II, interest in this subject has skyrocketed, due in large measure perhaps to the work of such men as C. S. Lewis. His book *The Screwtape Letters* brought a new consciousness of the work of Satan and his allies.

Demon worship in the form of magic, voodooism, witchcraft, divination, necromancy, and occultism (one or more of which may involve ouija boards, crystal balls, cartomancy, palmistry, rod and pendulum, psychometry, or other clairvoyant activities), together with Satanism, is fostered at present by men like Anton LaVey, founder of the first church of Satan in California over ten years ago. Many people have been caught up in some of these seemingly harmless practices, finding themselves immersed in the worship of demons or Satan before they realize the extent of their involvement.[99]

Titus Loong makes an interesting distinction between demon possession and demon oppression when he writes:

> A demon is not able to enter and control a man unless he consents to be controlled by the evil spirit. Advanced people observe less evidences of demon possession than do the primitives. This may be partly due to their more sophisticated minds, rejecting all kinds of superstitions, which help them to become less yielding to the evil spirits. However, another term, demon oppression, is applied to the state of being attacked or oppressed by an evil spirit without the voluntary will of man. It may therefore be simply stated that demon possession is from within, and demon oppression is from without. . . . A true Christian will not be possessed by demons, but he may be oppressed by Satan, the roaring lion that would not lose a single opportunity to damage the faith of a child of God.[100]

Using the case of the Gadarene demoniac described in Mark 5:1-20, paralleled in Luke 8:26-39, as the basis for observation, we may detail the following facts about demon possession:

A. The man was naked and had not worn clothes for a long time. When Jesus cast out the demons, the man clothed himself.

B. The man was a social outcast, for he lived in the tombs away from family and society. When the demons were cast out, Jesus bade him return to his house and to his city, and the man did so.

C. The demons recognized Jesus and used the man's voice to cry out, begging Jesus not to send them into the abyss. After the demons were expelled, the man had the normal use of his voice.

D. The demons caused the man to have great strength, for many times he broke the chains and shackles with which he was bound. When the demons were gone, the man sat calmly at Jesus' feet.

E. In paroxysms and fits of rage the man resisted Jesus, for the demons cried out in the man's voice, pleading not to be tormented, even though the man ran to Jesus and bowed down to Him. This indicates a disintegration of personality, implying a degree of insanity. He was in his "right mind" after Jesus cast out the demons.

F. Jesus commanded the demons to identify themselves. They responded with a definite name. This identification occurs in modern times when demons are cast out, as shown by many examples.

G. The demons were permitted to enter the swine, since it is important to demons that they inhabit some physical form, even if it is that of a pig (cf. Matthew 12:43-45; Luke 11:24-26).[101]

# 14

## *The Development of a Doctrine of Demonology*

Although the real existence of a spirit of evil is clearly revealed in the Bible, the revelation is made gradually in accord with the progressive method of God. In the first entrance of evil into the world, the temptation is external, through the serpent. All through the Old Testament the existence and nature of Satan remains in the background, perhaps felt, but not fully understood, with he possible exception of Job 1 and 2. It seems reasonable to assume, therefore, that the revelation of the great enemy against God is withheld until Christ, who is stronger than he, comes on the scene. Thus, in the first Gospel of the New Testament, we find Christ grappling with the tempter in the wilderness.

### *The origin of Old Testament demonology*

It was a common belief of the early Hebrews that the wide distance between God and man was filled with spiritual beings of varied descriptions. As some authorities have pointed out, it would be superfluous to "seek out, throughout all the texts of Scripture, all the interventions of the spirit of evil, such as they have been discovered by the innumerable theologians" who have studied the problem.[102]

Before Moses, hosts of divine spirits seemed to fill the entire universe, especially the human realm. The forces of nature and the shocks and changes of human history were all attributed to the power of spirits, good or bad. But these thoughts always led on toward God and did not diverge into polytheism as occurred in Egypt, Canaan, and Babylon.

During Moses' time and afterward the idea of the divine power at work in the world was reconciled with he knowledge that there was one God by regarding these powers as divine messengers or angels. These messengers became channels of revelation and led the way in difficult undertakings or shielded the godly from danger. At first, there was no distinction between good or bad angels. The bad spirit is said to be sent by God, but often this was no more than a bad disposition, such as in Judges 9:23, where it is said that "God sent an evil spirit (*ruach*) between Abimelech and the citizens of Shechem, who acted treacherously against Abimelech" (NIV).

Again, in 1 Samuel it is said that the "Spirit of the Lord had departed from Saul, and an evil spirit from the Lord tormented him" (1 Samuel 16:14 NIV). In this incident David, the son of Jesse, was called on to play his harp before Saul. This caused Saul to be refreshed and relieved of his melancholy or depression that resulted from his spiritual loss. The point is made that the Lord was given immediate connection with Saul's experience.

At a later date the evil spirit from God caused Saul to cast his javelin at David. Saul was jealous and full of rage because of David's popularity after slaying Goliath (1 Samuel 18:10-11). The messengers of God, on the other hand, were real spiritual beings who brought pestilence, stirred up men to war, and destroyed foes. Their forms were glorious; they came and went unexpectedly and spoke as heavenly prophets to people on earth. When the angel of the Lord appeared at times previously noted, those to whom he appeared usually did not recognize the fact immediately. Such was the case of Gideon (Judges 6:11-24).

In most cases the heavenly messengers visited singly, but in several instances more than one angel appeared. This was true in the angels' visit to Abraham and Lot before the destruction of Sodom. It was also true in places where the saints gathered for prayer or worship.

In the instances cited above it is clear that spirit beings, both good and bad, existed as definite realities in the literature and beliefs of the Hebrews. The Bible does not seek to prove the existence or discuss the origin of angels. Their existence is everywhere assumed in the Old Testament. It is also plainly stated that evil is permitted only as God allows it, as suggested in the following:

> •The Lord works out everything for his own ends — even the wicked for a day of disaster (Proverbs 16:4 NIV).

> •I am the Lord and there is no other, apart from me there is no God. . . . I form the light and create darkness, I bring prosperity and create disaster [evil]; I the Lord do all these things (Isaiah 45:5, 7 NIV).

> •Shall a trumpet be blown in the city, and the people not be afraid? Shall there be evil in a city, and the Lord hath not done it? (Amos 3:6 KJV).

The most obvious support for the existence and operation of evil spirits is made through the stern prohibitions and punishments of witchcraft. The following Scriptures make this clear:

> •Thou shall not suffer a witch to live (Exodus 22:18 KJV).

> •Let no one be found among you who sacrifices his son or daughter in the fire, who practices divination or sorcery, interprets omens, engages in witchcraft, or casts spells, or who is a medium or spiritist or who consults the dead. Anyone who does these things is detestable to the Lord, . . . (Deuteronomy 18:10-12 NIV).

> •. . . I saw the Lord sitting on his throne with all the host of heaven standing around him on his right and on his left. And the Lord said, "Who will lure Ahab into attacking Ramoth Gilead and going to his death there?" One suggested this and another that. Finally a spirit came forward, stood before the Lord and said,

> "I will lure him." "By what means?" the Lord asked. "I will go out and be a lying spirit in the mouths of all his prophets," he said. "You will succeed in luring him," said the Lord. "Go and do it" (1 Kings 22:19-22 NIV).

Although the last passage does not speak to the point of witchcraft, it serves to show that an evil spirit of lying came on the prophets of Ahab in order to defeat his wicked purposes against Israel. The tendency that Israel had to seek and consult the aid of evil spirits is also shown in the rebukes of the prophets such as Isaiah: "And when they say to you, 'Consult the mediums and the wizards who chirp and mutter,' should not a people consult their God? Should they consult the dead on behalf of the living?" (Isaiah 8:19 RSV).

Some writers make the attempt to connect the few resemblances of heathen demons in the Old Testament with Satan. During the Old Testament era a widespread belief prevailed that goatlike spirits roamed the fields and woods, the deserts, the ravines, and the mountains. These spirits were called *seirim.*[103] They appeared as hairy demons, also called satyrs, to whom sacrifice was made with fear and trembling. Disease and accident were attributed to evil spirits of the wilderness, and each type of disease or accident had its peculiar demon. For example, the well-known Beelzebub was the Philistine god of flies and illness, and Belial was the king of the nether world.[104]

Some have conjectured that the scapegoat of Leviticus 16 was connected with a desert or wilderness demon, named Azazel, that hid in the ravines near the city of Jerusalem and at the opening of each year a scapegoat was offered to him. No successful connection has ever been made at this point, however.[106]

One of the explanations for the origin of evil and of evil spirits — an explanation that is completely discounted by present day scholars — is found in the rabbinical writings and in apocalyptic literature. It concerns the account of Genesis 6, previously discussed, which identifies the "sons of God" (*elohim*) in

Genesis 6:2; Job 1:6; 2:1; 38:7 and interprets the phrase as demons or evil spirits, with the resulting union of fallen angels with the daughters of men.[106]

Another explanation of the existence of demons is that they were the last of all created beings. When the coming of the Sabbath interrupted their creation, they were left half angelic and half animal. They possessed the power of flight and they had intelligence, but they had the hearts of men and were utterly sensual. The union of these beings with the daughters of men resulted in offspring known as fallen angels.[107]

A much more palpable interpretation of the Genesis account is that the sons of *elohim* were the sons of Seth, being men of integrity, while the daughters of men were of disreputable character, possibly descended from Cain. The marriage of the two lines of human families then caused God to be concerned by the wickedness of the whole earth.

## New Testament demonology

When one moves from the Old Testament through the intertestamental period to the New Testament, the doctrine of an invisible evil agent becomes more and more clear. The mass of literature accumulated during the period between the Testaments is replete with references to evil spirits, demons, and Satan. Some authorities believe the influence of these writings on the New Testament is incontrovertible. Since such theories, now widely discounted, are also laced with references to Persian concepts of an earlier period, we must conclude that if any influence was exerted at all, it would have come through Hellenistic channels. Much of the literature of the intertestamental period was either written in or translated into the Greek language, which forms the indispensable bridge between the Testaments.

There is considerable material in the writings of the intertestamental period concerning the fall of angels and the origin of demons. Multitudes of evil spirits are pictured as being in constant antagonism to people. They cause physical evils and are represented as being the source of moral evil. With such references to evil spirits, we are better able to understand the emphasis given to the subject in the New Testament.

For the most part, the teaching concerning demons in the Jewish apocryphal literature is so closely connected with the teachings concerning angels that it is difficult to separate the two. This is especially true with regard to the fall of man and the fall of angels.

Enoch 6:1-15 relates how the angels saw and lusted after the daughters of men, and this passage may be a reflection of the record of Genesis 6:1-4, as the rabbis interpret it. In the days of Jared, two hundred angels are said to have descended to Mount Hermon, whereupon they took wives and sired great giants (Enoch 7:2). The motive of the descent is said to have been the satisfaction of lustful cravings, but in addition they imparted many kinds of knowledge to men and women. The result of the intercourse of angels with the human race was a great increase of lawlessness and bloodshed. A cry went up to heaven, and the four chief archangels, Michael, Uriel, Raphael, and Gabriel cried to God about the evil done by Azazel and his associates.

God sent Uriel to warn Noah of the coming deluge, while Raphael bound Azazel hand and foot and cast him into a dark place in the desert. There he is to remain bound until the day of judgment, when he will be cast into the lake of fire (Enoch 7:1-10).

The result of the whole experience of this unnatural intercourse between celestial spirits and human beings was the rise of a race of giants who gave birth to a brood of evil spirits. The exact meaning of this is not clear, but it may mean that the departed spirits of the giants are believed to have become malignant. According to Enoch, the evil spirits are free to carry on their operations against people and will not be punished until the day of judgment. There are other accounts of the fall of the angels and the origin of demons also. In Enoch 83-90, the angels are symbolized as stars. Enoch saw one bright star fall from heaven and later saw other stars cast themselves from heaven to join the first star.

In the book of Jubilees there are references to the fall of the angels, but their motive is said to have been to give instruction, direction, and upright judgment (Jub. 5:6). After their descent, however, the angels yielded to the seductions of women. Supposedly the fruit of these unions was the Naphidim (Jub. 7:22ff.), probably a parallel to the giants of Genesis 6:4. The demons then began to seduce the sons of Noah and their children (Jub. 7:27; 10:1ff.). Although much shorter, references in the Testaments of the Twelve Patriarchs are also made to the fall of angels and their subsequent imprisonment.

In Enoch 37-71 there are satans, in some sense regarded as evil spirits, who existed in heaven before the fall of the angels and who are responsible for that event. They are ruled by a chief named Satan, who has access to heaven.

In the Book of Adam and Eve is the story of the rebellion of Satan and his expulsion from heaven. Michael commanded the angels to worship Adam when God blew the breath of life into his nostrils. Satan refused to do so on the grounds that he was older than Adam and should himself be worshiped. Many of the angels under him also refused to worship Adam. God then hurled Satan and his angels down to earth. For this reason Satan set about to ruin Adam and Eve.[108]

A significant difference between the noncanonical literature of the intertestamental period and the New Testament is that in the latter Satan (the Devil) is the one great prince or chief, to whom all lesser evil powers are subordinate. For the most part, the apocryphal literature shows a decided belief in numerous chiefs of the fallen angels. Satan exists alongside Asmodaeus in the Book of Tobit, Semjaza and Azazel in 1 Enoch, Mastema in the Book of Jubilees, and Beliar in the Testaments of the Twelve Patriarchs; thus, although Satan is mentioned in some of the noncanonical literature, he is not prominent at all beside the other chiefs. The only possible parallel of this concept is the mention of Beelzebub and Beliar (Belial) in the New Testament (Matthew 10:25; 12:24, 27; Mark 3:22; Luke 11:15, 18-19; 2 Corinthians 6:15).

Without equivocation, Satan is the superhuman but created, real, evil, world-spirit power pictured in the New Testament as the adversary of both God and man. The two Greek names used most frequently in the New Testament for this great adversary are *satanas* and *diabolos*. The former is obviously a carry-over from the Hebrew *satan*. It is used in the Greek form a total of thirty-seven times and in every case except two it designates an *arch-fiend.*[109] The two exceptions are found in Matthew 16:23 and Mark 8:33, parallel texts in which Jesus rebuked Peter. The other texts include twelve in the Gospels, two in Acts, ten in the epistles of Paul and eight in the Apocalypse.[110]

*Diabolos* is used a total of thirty-five times in the New Testament, and in every case it is translated "devil" in the King James Version. In every case except one it is the Greek parallel of the Hebrew word *satan*. The single exception is in John 6:70, where Jesus said that of the twelve disciples He had chosen, one was a devil. The remaining thirty-four references include fourteen in the Gospels, two in Acts, twelve in the epistles, and six in the Book of Revelation.[111]

Rather positive proof that the two names were identical is given where both names are used in the same passage such as found in Matthew 4:1-10, where the names "Satan," "the devil," and "the tempter" are used synonymously; in Matthew 12:22-28, where "Beelzebub," "the prince of demons," and "Satan" are all identical; and in Revelation 20:1-3, where "the dragon," "ancient serpent," "the devil," and "Satan" are all used for the same deceiver of nations.

There are also passages in which the designations *demons*, *evil spirit*, and *evil spirits* are used synonymously and interchangeably, such as in the healing of the demoniac of Gadara, as told by Mark:

> A man with an evil spirit came from the tombs to meet him. . . . Jesus was saying to him, "Come out of this man, you evil spirit!"

> . . . The demons begged Jesus, "Send us among the pigs; . . . He gave them permission, and the evil spirits came out . . . (Mark 5:1-17, passim NIV).

The parallel of this incident is in Luke 8:26-39, where demons and evil/unclean spirits and devils are identical to each other.

Other forms of the Greek diabolos are used a total of seventy-nine times, usually translated "demon" in the King James Version. In addition to the two principal names of Satan and the Devil, a number of other names may also be noted. In two texts the Greek *peirazo*, meaning *to try* or *to prove*, is used. In both instances the word is translated "tempter" in the New International Version (Matthew 4:3; 1 Thessalonians 3:5).

Another proper name applied to Satan is Beelzebub, which transliterated from the Hebrew becomes Baal-Zebub. This is a compound word from Baal, meaning "a god," and Zebub, meaning "a fly." Thus the word means a "fly-god" or "god of the flies." This god was worshiped by the Philistines at Ekron, as described in 2 Kings 1:2. Jarrel notes that according to a better manuscript, the Jews changed the name from Baalzebub to Baalzebul. The name came to designate the Devil, probably "because he is the sinner's idol."[112]

Young states that this was "a heathen deity to whom the Jews ascribed supremacy among the evil spirits."[113] "Beelzebub" is used a total of seven times in the New Testament (Matthew 10:25; 12:24, 27; Mark 3:22; Luke 11:15, 18, 19). With the exception of the first reference listed, these are all parallels of the occasion on which Jesus was accused of casting out devils by the power of Beelzebub, the prince of the devils. It was on this occasion that Jesus asked how Satan could cast out Satan, thus showing that the Jews currently identified Satan as the prince of the devils.

Yet another identification is made in Matthew 13:39, where the only specific reference to Satan or the Devil as "the enemy" is found. Here the Devil is "the enemy" who sowed tares among the wheat while the men were sleeping. In the same text Jesus refers to "the wicked one" as the one who came and caught away what had been sown (Matthew 13:19). In verse 38, Jesus said that the tares are the children of "the wicked one." The same term is used by John (1 John 2:13-14; 3:12; 5:8).

The Greek *Beliar*, or Belial (2 Corinthians 6:15) indicates a "worthless" or "lawless" person and probably should not be taken as a proper noun. The best usage of the term associates it with a son, a daughter, or children; hence, "son" or "son of Belial" means a worthless person (in the moral sense) and is a transcript of the Hebrew, meaning "worthlessness" or "wickedness."[114]

In 1 Peter 5:8, the Devil is referred to as an enemy or adversary: "Be self-controlled and alert. Your enemy the devil prowls around like a roaring lion looking for someone to devour. Resist him" (NIV). A similar Pauline exhortation identifies Satan as the enemy-adversary: "So I counsel younger widows to marry, to have children, to manage their homes and to give the enemy no opportunity for slander. Some have in fact already turned away to follow Satan" (1 Timothy 5:14-15 NIV).

The Gospel of John indicates that the Devil is a murderer and the father of lies (John 8:44). Here Jesus stated that the Devil was the father of the hypocritical Pharisees, and that he was a murderer from the beginning. The Devil has no truth in him and when he speaks a lie, it is his own, for he is the father of lies. A further reference in 1 John 3:8 calls the Devil a sinner: "He who does what is sinful is of the devil, because the devil has been sinning from the beginning. The reason the Son of God appeared was to destroy the devil's work" (1 John 3:8 NIV).

A final reference to Satan and the various names applied to him is found in the Apocalypse, where one text combines all the names — "enormous red dragon," "the dragon," "the great dragon," "that ancient serpent," "the devil or Satan," "the accuser of our brothers," and "the serpent" — in describing the same malignant spirit (Revelation 12:1-17 NIV). In common with nearly all noncanonical apocalypses, the Book of Revelation contains considerable material on the subject of demonology and Satan.

The only specific passage in the Bible that declares that Satan is actually banished from heaven is the one cited in Revelation 12 (cf. Luke 10:18).

One of the most difficult passages in the whole of apocalyptic literature, Revelation 12:4, states that the dragon drew a third part of the stars of heaven and cast them to the earth. If this is the primeval war in heaven, then the stars must refer to angels, as Langton believes. He writes that the reference is "to the number of angels whom the dragon persuaded to become his followers, for stars are familiar symbols of fallen angels in Jewish literature."[115]

The passage also seems to indicate that Satan had access to heaven until the time described. The problem is centered on what time the reference indicates. It may well be that the best solution is to interpret the statement in a reflective or a retroactive manner, so that once cast out, Satan has no further access to heaven. His casting out was violent and Satan's activity seems to be limited to the earth at this time. He is no longer allowed access to God or to heaven.

Satan is also pictured as being in a great rage when cast to earth from heaven. After this time, there occurs a great tribulation on the earth, but Satan is bound and cast into the pit, where he is held for one thousand years. At the end of this period Satan is released for a short time, whereupon he gathers an army for a last all-out assault on the people of God. Upon being defeated, he is thrown into the lake of fire, where he meets his final doom, since the fire burns forever and ever. These events are pictured in Revelation 19 and 20.

Thus the origin and history of Satan can be set forth only in the most general terms, since there is no genesis of the Devil in the New Testament. Having no description of his birth or creation, the assumption throughout the New Testament, as well as the whole Bible, is simply that he stands near, if not behind, all human sinning, not as relieving the sinner of his responsibility, but as coagent with him and as the very essence of all evil.[116]

Two other New Testament texts show the sufficiency of the power of God over Satan and the fallen angels, in past history as well as in prophetic utterance, as follows:

- For if God did not spare angels when they sinned, but cast them into hell and committed them to pits of darkness, reserved for judgment . . . (2 Peter 2:4).
- And He [Jesus] said to them, "I was watching Satan fall from heaven like lightning" (Luke 10:18).

The last reference is to the time when the seventy, whom Jesus had sent out, returned and were joyful because even the demons were subject to them.

## *The works and kingdom of Satan*

The world-wide and age-long works of Satan can be traced to one prevailing motive. He hates both God and man and does all within his power to defeat the plan of God in order to establish his own kingdom of evil. His overshadowing motive seems to be that of gaining equality with God through the means of deception.

Since Satan's work is to pervert the things of God, this perversion is extended to the conception of the kingdom as well. "Satan's ambition is leading him to make this age of his special opportunity . . . [a time when] the Satanic ideal of this age is [realized] . . . with people who are devout worshipers of himself."[117] As there is a kingdom of God, so also there is a kingdom of Satan. Stevens observes that the popular thought of Jesus' time "attributed the power of evil, both natural and moral, to the agency of wicked spirits."[118] These spirits were thought of as constituting a kingdom of evil of which Satan is the head. These malignant powers are perpetually active in bringing all manner of evil upon people and are referred to as principalities, powers, and rulers of darkness (Ephesians 6:12 KJV). This can only indicate that there is an organization of evil forces under the headship of the "prince of the world," whom Jesus mentions as being cast out (John 12:31), as having nothing in Him (14:30), and as being judged (16:11).

That there are a great number of evil spirits under the leadership of Satan is indicated by various Scripture passages such as Mark 5:9 "My name is legion" (KJV) and by the reference to the lake of fire prepared for the devil and his angels (Matthew 25:41 KJV). When the man from Gadara came to Jesus, all the demons begged Him to send them into the herd of swine (Mark 5:12). It is also said that when an unclean spirit is gone out of a man, it cannot find rest, so it determines to return to its former abode. Upon finding it swept, clean, and empty, the spirit finds seven other spirits even more wicked and the whole group enters the man, making his last state worse than the first (Matthew 12:43-45).

John 8:44; 2 Peter 2:4; and Jude 6 give further evidence of the hosts of Satan. Although their origin cannot be traced, these beings are pictured as being bodiless spirits who make up at least a portion of Satan's kingdom. It is also obvious that these devils are seeking to enter the bodies of human people or beasts, for their power is in some sense dependent on such possession. In one instance men who were possessed with devils were brought to Jesus and "he cast out the spirits with his word, and healed all that were sick" (Matthew 8:16 KJV). In Matthew 8:28 it may be observed that the devils are wicked, unclean, and vicious. Two men possessed by demons are described as being "so exceedingly violent that no one could pass by that road." Other texts also show the vicious character of the demons as well as their purpose to possess a human person or a beast (Mark 5:2-5 RSV; Mark 9:20 KJV; Acts 8:7; 16:16-18).

From the passages immediately cited, it may also be inferred that there are degrees of wickedness represented by these evil beings. Their influence seems to vary with the persons they possess, as prompted by the motives of hindering the purposes of God and in extending the kingdom of Satan. The devils cooperate willingly at the command of their chief and recognize the authority and deity of Christ, as seen in other passages of Scripture (Matthew 8:29; Luke 4:33-34; Acts 16:13-16; James 2:19).

Concerning the Devil's work, it may be noted that he is referred to as a "thief" and a "hireling" (John 10:10, 12); he drove the

Gadarene demoniac into the desert (Luke 8:29); he is the sower of tares (Matthew 13:25, 28-29); he takes the word out of human hearts (Matthew 13:19; Luke 8:12); he tempts people to do evil (Matthew 4:1-10; Luke 4:1-8); he bound a woman for eighteen years (Luke 13:16); and he seeks the human heart as a place to do his evil work (Luke 22:3, 31).

Satan also has direct control over his subjects and has great power and authority during this age, as suggested in Acts 10:38, and even over death (Hebrews 2:14). The exact limits of his power, under the restraining hand of God, cannot be known, but it would be reasonable to conclude, as does Chafer, that he is the god of this age, the head of the great world system of evil, and the director of the affairs of "unregenerate men."[119] The motive of Satan is finalized in the assumption of the role of "the man of lawlessness" (2 Thessalonians 2:3-4, 7-12).

The churches of Smyrna and Philadelphia are said to have members who belong to the synagogue of Satan (Revelation 2:9, 3:9), while those of Thyatira are told that there are those among them who have "known the deep things of Satan" (Revelation 2:24). This seems to indicate that John and Paul have both written the same truth about Satan and the system he propagates. The poignant warnings of Paul seem to bear this out (2 Corinthians 11:13-15; 1 Timothy 4:1-2).

Considering all the above Scriptures, it is obvious that Satan is the instigator and fomenter of the spirit of lawlessness that exhibits itself as hatred, both of the truth and light, which has operated so widely, universally, and disastrously in the human family.

Having noted numerous passages of Scripture that deal with the existence and operation of Satan and his evil hosts, we can make a number of observations. First, the existence of Satan and numerous evil spirits is clearly assumed in the New Testament, although their origin is not discussed. Second, the use of the word *daimon* reaches its final stage in the New Testament and always signifies an evil-working spirit. Third, the number of evil spirits is indefinitely large, as many references make clear. This is also true of the intertestamental apocalypses and other noncanonical Jewish literature, though we cannot place such records on the same level as the inspired revelation of God in the books of the canon. In the synoptic Gospels the evil work of demons seems to be largely physical rather than moral.

Again, it may be noted that demons are associated with definite localities — such as deserts, tombs, mountains, and desolate and waterless places — and with wild beasts. Jesus was tempted in a wilderness or solitary place. Furthermore, certain references such as Matthew 12:45 and Luke 11:26 seem to imply that evil spirits move in groups. Seven evil spirits are mentioned as working or dwelling together, and seven demons were cast out of Mary Magdalene. Finally, the New Testament shows that evil spirits produce a great variety of evil effects in the lives of human individuals.

It also seems reasonable to believe that Jesus accepted the teaching that prevailed among the Jews of His day concerning the existence and operation of evil spirits or demons. Not for a moment did He hesitate to face the demons squarely and to command them to come out of people. Mark especially pictures Jesus as the great "Deliverer," who delivers from death, disabilities of every kind, destruction, and demons. The very presence of Jesus terrified the demons, who at His command left their victims.

The belief of Jesus in the existence of Satan, as the head of the kingdom of evil, is equally evident from the Gospel accounts. Langton makes the following pertinent observation:

> It is impossible to suppose that Jesus merely pretended to a belief in Satan and the demons without casting a very grave reflection upon His character as a teacher. Such pretense, moreover, would be out of accord with the whole impression of sincerity made upon us by His life and work.[120]

## *Beliefs and teachings about Satan and demons through the ages*

It is far beyond the scope of this study to review all the varied ideas that churchmen have projected. The least that can be noted is that throughout the history of Christianity there is an unbroken line of ardent believers in the existence of Satan and demons, as well as demon possession and the casting out of demons by the power of God.

## *The first eight centuries of the Christian era*

The apostolic and early church fathers, quite generally continued to carry on the teachings of the first-century Christians and writers. In the writings of Justin Martyr, Tatian, Irenaeus, Tertullian, Origen, Cyprian, Eusebius, Ambrose of Milan, Chrysostom, Jerome, Augustine, Gregory the Great, and John of Damascus demonology had a significant place. By far the greatest influence in the thought of the early church was wielded by Tertullian (*ca.* A.D. 155-230), Origin (*ca.* A.D. 185-254) Eusebius (264-340), and Augustine (*ca.* A.D. 354-430). Tertullian wrote so profusely on the subject that one would almost conclude he was obsessed with demons, who were fallen angels, and with Satan, who is the chief of the demons. To Tertullian they wee endowed with great swiftness and were both invisible and intangible. Any person who could not expel a demon was not to be regarded as a genuine Christian, according to Tertullian.

Origen had the most elaborate demonology of any writer up to his time. He was also bold to suggest novel ideas such as the possibility of the salvation of the devil and his angels by the discipline of the future world. He did not, however, believe that fallen angels were demons, although he did not suggest what their identities were. To Origen, all pagan gods were really demons and he asserted that demons had bodies, however unlike humans they were. Demons also embodied animals in order to stir them up and make them ferocious, with each species of demons having an affinity with a given noxious type of animal.

Eusebius especially followed Porphyry and Plutarch in much of what he believed. Thus he thought demons were subject to death and that all gods of the pagans were demons. Demons are found everywhere, according to Eusebius, and they especially delight in being close to human beings, most of all delighting in blood and impure meat.

Augustine is thought to have fixed the doctrines and teachings of the Western church for a thousand years on many subjects, including his views of the Devil and demons. His interpretation of Genesis 6:1-2 is that the sons of Seth (not angels or demons) made the daughters of Cain bear giants. Demons had bodies, Augustine said, but they were not material. They lived in the air but they were in no sense intermediaries between God and the human race. He associated demons with magic, magicians, and necromancy and held that they could even assault infants. If they possessed a human person, it was always by deceit and guile. They are expelled by the sacrifice of Christ and by the power of God's Holy Spirit.

## *Demonology from the Middle Ages to Wesley*

Numerous references are made to Satan and the demons in scholastic literature and that of the monastic orders. Anselm (1033-1109), Bernard (1090-1153), Peter Lombard (1100-1160), and Thomas Aquinas (1227-1274) all spoke to the issue, Aquinas being the most influential. His views are still held to be authoritative in the Roman Catholic church. Aquinas believed that the Devil probably rebelled almost immediately after his creation and that the demons are fallen angels who followed him. He defined demons as intellectual substances for whom there is no hope of salvation. Demons perform a useful service to human beings in tempting, testing, and proving them. God permits them to do this but He is always in control over them. They cannot work miracles in the strict sense of the word.

Martin Luther (1483-1546) was a thoroughgoing believer in the Devil and demons. If the story of the ink spots on the wall at the castle of Wartburg is apocryphal, it is nevertheless in perfect accord with Luther's views. He accepted most of the crude beliefs that had grown up during the Middle Ages. He thought the Devil was in control of the world, including the woods, the waters, and the deserts, where demons dwell. The demons are in the clouds and cause hail, thunder, and lightning. They cause people to walk in their sleep and frighten people with dreams and visions. The Devil is in control of witches, who spoil eggs, milk, and butter, in order to harass and annoy human beings. Luther distinguished between corporeal and spiritual types of possession, the latter being the more serious, since such cases are hopeless. Corporeal possession does not lend one's soul to the power of Satan or the demons, Luther said.

John Calvin (15090-1564) left most of the crude medieval ideas about demons out of his demonology but held rigidly to biblical interpretations. One of the emphasis for which Calvin is noted is his respect for prophetic reserve, for God has not seen fit to reveal all the mysteries of iniquity, and we must be satisfied that He is in control. The Bible is silent on many questions we might ask, and we must also be silent and use discretion.

Joseph Hall (1574-1656) and Richard Baxter (1615-1691) form a link between the Reformation period and John Wesley. Hall, Baxter, and Wesley all had firm beliefs regarding Satan and demons. Baxter followed Luther in his ideas, rather than Calvin, and Hall seems to have shaken many of the crudities from his demonology.[121]

## *Demonology from Wesley to the present*

John Wesley (1703-1791) stands in a long line of scholars who passed the thought patterns of their age to the next generation. One should not be surprised at some of the views he held with regard to ghosts and witches if the atmosphere of his time is kept in view. Evil angels for Wesley were those who were created pure and good, but did not keep their "first estate." If they were not wholly immaterial, Wesley believed that at least they did not have earthly, human flesh and blood. There is nothing we can know about the angels, either the good and pure or the fallen, wicked ones, he said, except through revelation.

Wesley did not know what caused the fall of the angels but he believed they are now full of pride, haughtiness, and greed. The evil angels are united under one head, Satan, and they are organized in various orders and assigned offices and work to carry out. They are always warring against the human race, with supernatural knowledge, taking every opportunity to wreak havoc by infusing evil thoughts into people's minds, rousing their passions and darkening their hearts. The Devil is responsible for many ills and diseases. He causes horses to be frightened; carriages to overturn; bones to be broken or dislocated; houses to burn; and damages to be done by lightning, hail, snow, wind, or rain. The Devil also causes little inconveniences, such as the breaking of a bench on which we are sitting.[122]

Wesley held orthodox views (those that had been generally accepted and little changed through the ages from the early church fathers to his time) concerning demons and their possession of human beings.[123] He was also firmly of the opinion that witches were wicked cohorts of Satan and should be burned. He wrote, "With my latest breath will I bear my testimony against giving up to infidels one great proof of the invisible world: I mean, that of Witchcraft and apparitions, confirmed by the testimony of all ages."[124] On numerous occasions, Wesley makes reference to strange and inexplicable phenomena and simply leaves them unexplained.

Schleiermacher (1768-1834) found considerable difficulty in accepting the traditional view concerning Satan. He reasoned that if Satan and his angels wee created perfectly pure — with superior intelligence, wisdom, and insight — it is impossible to see how they could fall, for then evil would exist side by side with God's purity; their insight should show the futility of going against God, unless Satan's error was due to a lack of intelligence. He found as much difficulty regarding angels that fell as regarding those who did not. Schleiermacher also contends that neither Jesus nor any of His apostles ever said anything about Satan or the demons that was different from what was current in their time. They also made no connection of the Devil with salvation. In key passages on the subject of sin — *e.g.*, Romans 1-8 and James 1 — there is no mention of Satan. Therefore, the matter of Satan's existence is a subject for cosmology rather than for theology.

From the time of Schleiermacher to the present there have been many scholars who have followed his reasoning and do not take the concept of Satan at face value. Even so, the church has retained the ideas of Satan and angels, good or bad, for poetic use such as in Christian hymnology.[125] Not until W. B. Pope championed the traditional belief in angels, Satan, and demons in his three volumes published in 1880, did the philosophically oriented views of Schleiermacher and others who followed him begin to be seen in different perspective. Whatever the influence of Pope as a Methodist theologian may have been, many theologians of the late nineteenth and early twentieth centuries made little or no mention of Satan at all, including J. S. Banks, W. N. Clarke, James Denney, A. S. Peake, and J. S. Whale.

From a period in which Satan and demons were considered to be relics of past superstitions, the middle decades of the twentieth century to the present decade of the eighties have seen a plethora of books showing that Satan and his demons are not dead. The existential evidence from around the world with regard to demons and demon possession is altogether too vast to ignore, especially since much of this evidence corroborates the biblical evidence. C. S. Lewis places the accent squarely where it should be in Screwtape's seventh letter to Wormwood:

> I wonder you should ask me whether it is essential to keep the patient in ignorance of your own existence. That question, at least for the present phase of the struggle, has been answered for us by the High Command. Our policy for the moment is to conceal ourselves. Of course this has not always been so. We are really faced with a cruel dilemma. When the humans disbelieve in our

> existence we lose all the pleasing results of direct terrorism and we make no magicians. On the other hand, when they believe in us, we cannot make them materialists and skeptics. At least not yet. I have great hopes that we shall learn in due time how to emotionalize and mythologise their science to such an extent that what is, in effect, a belief in us, (though no under that name) will creep in while the human mind remains closed to belief in the Enemy. The "Life Force," the worship of sex, and some aspects of Psychoanalysis, may here prove useful.[126]

Lewis explains the force of his insight as follows:

> There are two equal and opposite errors into which our race can fall about the devils. One is to disbelieve in their existence. The other is to believe, and to feel an excessive and unhealthy interest in them. They themselves are equally pleased by both errors and hail a materialist or a magician with the same delight.[127]

1. C. Fred Dickason, *Angels, Elect and Evil* (Chicago: Moody, 1975), p.17.
2. Bernard Ramm, "Angels," in *Basic Christian Doctrines*, ed. Carl F. H. Henry (Grand Rapids: Baker, 1973), p. 63.
3. John Macartney Wilson, "Angel," in *International Standard Bible Encyclopaedia* (hereinafter ISBE), ed. James Orr, 5 vols. (Grand Rapids: Eerdmans, 1947), 1:132.
4. Charles W. Carter, ed., *Wesleyan Bible Commentary*, 6 vols. (Grand Rapids: Eerdmans, 1967), 1:70-75 (notes on Genesis 18-19); 1:108-10 (notes on Genesis 32:22-32); 1:178 (notes on Exodus 3:1-12).
5. John Wesley, *Explanatory Notes Upon the Old Testament*, 3 vols. (Salem, Ohio; Schmul, 1975), 3:2576-2581. See also 1:86-87 (notes on Genesis 22:11-15); 1:797-98 (notes on Judges 2:1); 1:817 (notes on Judges 6:21).
6. A.B. Davidson, *Theology of the Old Testament* (New York: Scribner, 1906), p. 213.
7. Dickason, *Angels, Elect and Evil*, pp. 80-81.
8. Wilson, "Angel," in *ISBE*, 1:134.
9. See Adam Clarke's comment and John Wesley's note on Job 38:7, where the context hardly allows "sons of God" to be symbolic of the spheres, as some writers suggest. The "morning stars" that "sang together" may quite naturally in accord with the context be understood to be planets or other celestial bodies. It is consistent with this context, which throughout its emphasis is far back in the cosmic order, to interpret "sons of God" as preadamic. Thus from any logical perspective the phrase may refer to created spiritual beings, *i.e.*, the angelic hosts, as Clarke and Wesley conclude. For alternate views see Keil & Delitzsch, *Commentary on the Book of Job* (Grand Rapids: Eerdmans, n.d.), 2:311-15; and *The Wesleyan Bible Commentary*, 2:155.
10. H. Orton Wiley and Paul T. Culbertson, *Introduction to Christian Theology* (Kansas City, Mo.: Beacon Hill, 1946), p. 144.
11. Ibid.
12. Mrs. George C. Needham, *Angels and Demons* (Chicago: Moody, 1963), p. 19.
13. The Council of Nicea held that angels had bodies of ether or light. The Lateran Council, A.D. 1215, declared that angels were incorporeal (See Charles Hodge, *Systematic Theology* [New York: Scribner, 1893]), 1:637-38. During the Middle Ages the church came to the conclusion that angels are pure spiritual beings. Even so, some Roman Catholic, Lutheran, and Arminian theologians, along with Reformed scholars, ascribe a certain degree of corporeity to angels. (See L. Berkhof, *Systematic Theology* [Grand Rapids: Eerdmans, 1941]), p.144.

14. Geoffrey W. Bromiley, "Angel," in *Baker's Dictionary of Theology* (hereinafter BDT), ed. Everett F. Harrison (Grand Rapids: Baker, 1960, p. 41.
15. Elizabeth A. Livingstone, ed., *The Concise Oxford Dictionary of the Christian Church*, (London: Oxford University Press, 1977), p. 20.
16. Billy Graham, *Angels: God's Secret Agents* (New York: Doubleday, 1975), pp. 49-58, passim.
17. Dickason, *Angels, Elect and Evil*, p. 61.
18. Ibid., pp. 61-77, passim.
19. Needham, *Angels and Demons*, pp. 22-23.
20. Gabriel, whose name means "God is mighty," is named only four times in the Bible; *viz.*, Daniel 8:16; 9:21; Luke 1:19, 26. Michael is the only one of the two named angels in the Bible who is called an archangel (in Jude 9), with even the term *archangel* being used only one other time in Scripture (1 Thessalonians 4:16). Michael is named in only four places besides Jude 9; namely, Daniel 10:13, 21; 12:1; Revelation 12:7. His name means "Godlike," or "Who is like God?"
21. This may possibly be a reference to the awe, the reverence, and respect with which the angels come into the presence of God, and to the fact that they would be dismayed to see the lack of respect and perhaps modesty in the context of Paul's day, if women, the highest of the human race, the crowning glory of man, were improper in their approach to God. It is also probable that the early Christians, taking a cue from later Judaism, thought that angels were present in the worship services along with the Father, Son, and Holy Spirit, as well as the human worshipers. Since women were to be subordinate to all others, this directive was given to avoid any conflict, in all probability. See Charles W. Carter, *The Wesleyan Bible Commentary*, 5:191-92. See also Ralph Earle, *Word Meanings in the New Testament* (Grand Rapids: Baker, 1979), 4:67.
22. The Angel of the Lord in intimate association with a divine personality, is an obvious example. Joshua 5:13-15 may also be such an exception, although a clear reference to the Angel of the Lord is not made.
23. Bromiley, "Angel," in *BDT*, pp. 41ff.
24. Roy A. Stewart, "Angel," in *The New International Dictionary of the Christian Church* (hereinafter NIDCC), ed. J. D. Douglas (Grand Rapids: Zondervan, 1974), p. 42.
25. St. Thomas Aquinas, *Summa Theologiae* (New York: McGraw-Hill, 1970), 15:3
26. Stewart, "Angel," *NIDCC*, p. 42.
27. Heppe, *Reformed Dogmatics*, pp. 201-19, cited in *NIDCC*, p. 42.
28. Bromiley, "Angel," *BDT*, p. 43.
29. H. Martensen, *Christian Dogmatics, A Compendium of the Doctrines of Christianity*, tr. from the German by William Urwick (Edinburgh: T. & T. Clark, 1878), pp. 135-36.
30. Pie-Raymond Regamey, *What Is an Angel?* tr. from the French by Mark Pontifex (New York: Hawthorn, 1960), p. 9, citing Rudolph Bultmann in *The Theology of the New Testament*.
31. *The Works of The Rev. John Wesley* (London: John Mason, 1840), 7:222.
32. Ibid.
33. Ibid., 10:99-100.
34. Ibid., 10:100. (See also and compare Section III, pp. 140-41.)

35. Ibid., 6:341.
36. Ibid., p. 342.
37. Ibid., p. 344.
38. Ibid., p. 346-47.
39. Ibid., p. 347.
40. Ibid., p. 349.
41. Ibid., p. 346.
42. Ibid., p. 349.
43. Ibid., p. 389.
44. Aquinas, *Summa Theologize*, 15:49-71, passim.
45. Regamey, *What is an Angel?* p. 91.
46. Ibid., p. 95.
47. Livingstone, *Concise Oxford Dictionary*, p. 226.
48. Luther Lee, *Elements of Theology or an Exposition of the Origin, Doctrines, Morals and Institutions of Christianity* (Syracuse, N. Y.; A. W. Hall, 1899), p. 227.
49. The Scripture passages cited in this paragraph are from the RSV.
50. John Miley, *Systematic Theology* (New York: Methodist Book Concern, 1894), 2:490.
51. Genesis 28:12; Nehemiah 9:6; Psalm 148:2-5; Luke 15:10; John 1:1-3; Romans 8:38; Ephesians 1:31; 6:12; Colossians 1:16; 1 Timothy 6:16; Hebrews 1:6; 1 Peter 3:22; Revelation 4:11.
52. J. Stafford Wright, *Man in the Process of Time* (Grand Rapids: Eerdmans, 1956), p. 126.
53. Some Roman Catholic, Arminian, and even Lutheran and Reformed scholars ascribe to angels a degree of corporeity, most pure and subtle. See L. Berkhof, *Systematic Theology*, p. 144.
54. Martensen, *Christian Dogmatics*, pp. 127-28. See also, Regamey, *What Is an Angel?* p. 36.
55. Henry C. Thiessen, *Introductory Lectures on Systematic Theology* (Grand Rapids: Eerdmans, 1977), pp. 192-93.
56. Miley, *Systematic Theology*, 2:492.
57. It should be noted that the words used in Scripture that are translated "messenger" or "angel," are used in at least five different and distinct ways: (1) as ordinary human messengers (Job 1:14); (2) as applied to John the Baptist, the forerunner of Jesus and angel of the covenant (Malachi 3:1); (3) as designations for spiritual leaders of churches (Revelation 1:20; (4) as an impersonal agent in the case of Paul's thorn in the flesh (2 Corinthians 12:7); (5) as the heavenly intelligences, or spirit beings, that are the real subject of our consideration (Matthew 25:31; Hebrews 1:14; 2:7).
58. Graham, *Angels: God's Secret Agents*, pp. 49-50.
59. The Apocrypha enumerates six angels of power, whom some believe are to be considered archangels by ancient writers of the first or second century B.C., *viz.* Uriel, Raphael, Raguel, Michael, Zariel, and Gabriel. A seventh name is included as a variant reading in the margin as Remiel (Enoch 20:1-7). Tobit 12:15 gives the following additional comment: "I am Raphael, one of the seven holy angels who offer up prayers of the saints, and enter in before the glory of the Holy One."
60. Dickason, *Angels, Elect and Evil*, p. 63.

61. John Milton, The Harvard Classics, "Paradise Lost," ed. Charles W. Eliot (New York: Collier, 1909), p. 91.
62. Merrill F. Unger, *Demons in the World Today* (Wheaton: Tyndale, 1971), p. 10.
63. A most interesting and enlightening Master of Religion Thesis, "Magic and Its Influence on Primitive Medicine," was written by Lois E. Sheridan at Marion College, Marion, Indiana, 1950, prior to her first term as a medial missionary to Sierra Leone, West Africa. The former Miss Sheridan, now Mrs. Malcolm Ellis, indicated that her study served as a ballast against the culture shock experienced by many who go to the mission field without preparation or understanding of demons and evil spirits.
64. Charles W. Carter, "the Validity of the Concept of Soul in Animistic and Ancient Thought," Master of Theology thesis, Butler University Graduate School of Religion, now Christian Theological Seminary, Indianapolis, Indiana. This is a comprehensive study of the soul from animistic, Greek, Semitic, Egyptian, and Roman concepts, with a final study of the teachings of Christ concerning the soul.
65. For support of the progressive development of the concept of Satan, it must be assumed that the Books of Samuel were written before the Books of Kings, that Job precedes Zechariah, that both Job and Zechariah were written after the Books of Samuel and Kings and that the Books of Chronicles were written last of all the books mentioned.
66. John M'Clintock and James Strong, *Cyclopaedia of Biblical, Theological, and Ecclesiastical Literature*, s.v. "Satan" (New York: Harper and Brothers, 1894), 9:360.
67. Albert C. Knudson, *The Religious Teaching of the Old Testament* (New York: Abingdon, 1918), p. 210.
68. A. B. Davidson, *The Theology of the Old Testament* (New York: Scribner, 1906), p. 300.
69. Robert Young, *Analytical Concordance to the Bible* (New York: Funk & Wagnalls, n.d.).
70. Thirteen of these cases are in the Book of Job: Job 1:6, 7 (twice), 8, 9, 12 (twice); 2:1, 2 (twice), 3, 6, 7; two are in Zechariah (3:1, 2), one in 1 Chronicles 21:1, and one in Psalm 109:6. The word is transliterated without being translated in the KJV.
71. Louis Matthew Sweet, "Satan," ISBE, 9:360.
72. See also John 8:44; 2 Corinthians 11:3, 14; and Revelation 20:2.
73. John Wesley, *Explanatory Notes Upon the New Testament* (Naperville, Ill.: Alec R. Allenson, 1966), p. 996.
74. John P. Newport, "Satan and Demons: A Theological Perspective," in *Demon Possession*, ed. John Warwick Montgomery (Minneapolis: Bethany Fellowship, 1976), p. 326.
75. Ibid.
76. Lee M. Haines, "Genesis," in *The Wesleyan Bible Commentary*, 1:35.
77. Dennis F. Kinlaw, "The Demythologization of the Demonic in the Old Testament," in Montgomery, *Demon Possession*, p. 35.
78. Ibid.
79. Adam Clarke, *A Commentary and Critical Notes* (New York: Abingdon-Cokesbury, n.d.), 1:47-50.
80. Wiley and Culbertson, *Introduction to Christian Theology*, pp. 160-61.

81. Oscar Cullman, *Christ and Time* (Philadelphia: Westminster, 1964), p. 198. Cullman cites Mark 3:27 in support of Satan's being bound. He is not powerless, but his power has been broken, limited, or qualified. He is bound but with "a long rope."
82. Wittaker Chambers, "The Devil," *Life Magazine*, 24 (February 2, 1948), pp. 84-85.
83. Wright, *Man in the Process of Time*, pp. 128-31.
84. *Wesleyan Bible Commentary*, 1:44-45; 2:27-30, 154-55.
85. Wesley, *Explanatory Notes Upon the Old Testament*, 1:29; 2:1, 518-19, 1,611.
86. Among those who espouse this view are G. Campbell Morgan, Lewis Sperry Chafer, John J. Owen, A. C. Gaebelein, A. H. Strong, A. A. Hodge, and Charles Hodge.
87. Thiessen, *Introductory Lectures in Systematic Theology*, p. 201.
88. Ibid. For an extended discussion of the use of "sons of God," as used in Genesis 6:2; Job 1:6; 2:1; 38:7, as well as a discussion of Satan and evil spirits in general see C. F. Keil and F. Delitzsch, *Biblical Commentary on the Old Testament* (Grand Rapids: Eerdmans, 1971), 1:127-35. Here it is underscored that philology alone is not adequate for a correct interpretation. Contextual and theological considerations must also be weighed, which Charles W. Carter also insists on in his extra traditional view that Job's family may well have been included, along with others, in the phrase, "sons of God," with no logical reason why Satan should gain entrance into a heavenly court from which he had been cast out. See also, *Beacon Bible Commentary*, 10 vols. (Kansas City, Mo.; Beacon Hill, 1974), 1:52-53; 3:28-29; and John Peter Lange, *Commentary on the Holy Scriptures: Critical, Doctrinal and Homiletical* (Grand Rapids: Zondervan, n.d.), 1:280-82.
89. Flavius Josephus, *Wars of the Jews*, 7:6:3.
90. Thiessen, *Introductory Lectures in Systematic Theology*, pp. 200-201.
91. Some of those who support this view include G. H. Pember, Clarence Larkin, John L. Nevius, Ford C. Ottman, and George P. Pardington. Cf., also, the treatment given to this subject by Thiessen, *Introductory Lectures*, p. 201; Merrill F. Unger, *Biblical Demonology* (Wheaton, Ill.: Scripture, 1963), pp. 42-45; and Dickason, *Angels, Elect and Evil*, pp. 151-57.
92. John Peter Lange, "Genesis," *Commentary on the Holy Scriptures* (New York: Scribner, 1865), pp. 280-84.
93. Unger, *Biblical Demonology*, pp. 46-47.
94. Keil and Delitzsch, *Biblical Commentary on the Old Testament*, 1:127-35.
95. Unger, *Biblical Demonology*, pp 40-41.
96. T. Witton Davies, *Magic, Divination, and Demonology Among the Hebrews and Their Neighbors* (London: James Clarke, 1898), p. 103.
97. Luther Lee, *Elements of Theology or An Exposition of the Divine Origin, Doctrines, Moral and Institutions of Christianity* (Syracuse, N. Y.: A. W. Hall, 1899), p. 224.
98. J. H. Thayer, *Greek-English Lexicon of the New Testament*.
99. *Demon Experiences in Many Lands*, compiled by Kenneth N. Taylor (Chicago: Moody, 1960). See also Montague Summers, The History of Witchcraft and Demonology (London: Routledge & Kegan Paul, 1969), and Dickason, Angels, Elect and Evil, pp. 196-209.
100. Titus Loong, "Evidences for Psycho-Physical Disorders and Their Remedies in the Gospels and the Acts," a thesis written for the Master of Divinity degree, China Evangelical Seminary, Charles W. Carter, Faculty Advisor, 1974, pp. 47-48.

101. Dickason, *Angels, Elect and Evil*, p. 185.
102. Maurice Garcon and Jean Vinchon, *The Devil* (New York: Dutton, 1930), p. 21.
103. K. Kohler, *Jewish Theology* (New York: Macmillan, 1923), p. 190.
104. Ibid.
105. Davidson, *Theology of the Old Testament*, p. 304.
106. Kohler, *Jewish Theology*, p. 191.
107. Ibid., pp. 191-92.
108. Edward Langton, *Essentials of Demonology* (London: Epworth, 1949), pp. 118-19.
109. W. A. Jarrel, *The Devil* (Dallas: Published by the Author, 1908), pp. 48-49.
110. Young, *Analytical Concordance*.
111. Ibid.
112. Jarrell, *The Devil*, p. 49.
113. Young, *Analytical Concordance*.
114. Marvin R. Vincent, *Word Studies in the New Testament* (Grand Rapids: Eerdmans, 1946), 3:325.
115. Langton, *Essentials of Demonology*, p. 217.
116. Henry C. Sheldon, *New Testament Theology* (New York: Macmillan, 1911), p. 331.
117. Lewis Sperry Chafer, *Satan* (Chicago: Bible Institute Colportage Association, 1935), p. 75.
118. George Barker Stevens, *The Theology of the New Testament* (New York: Scribner, 1911), p. 82.
119. Chafer, *Satan*, p. 57.
120. Langton, *Essentials of Demonology*, p. 223.
121. For an excellent review of the character and work of Satan and demons through the ages, see Edward Langton, *Satan, A Portrait* (London: Skeffington, 1977), pp. 9-122. Much of the material summarized in the history of Satan from the first eight centuries of the Christian era, through the Middle Ages, to Wesley is based on Langton's study.
122. *The Works of John Wesley*, Sermon LXXII, "Of Evil Angels" (London: John Mason, 1840), 6:350-60, passim.
123. Ibid., 14:304.
124. Ibid., pp. 307ff. See also 10:41-44.
125. In a survey of approximately 3,000 hymns, gospel songs and choruses, made by the writer's daughter, Joy A. Caldwell — Abilene, Kansas, Middle School music teacher — the following data were collected: 304 hymns, gospel songs, or choruses included angels by name 221 times in 196 different songs, with the use of seraph(im/s) 14 times; cherub(im/s) 8 times; Gabriel 3 times; messenger(s), definitely referring to angels, twice; archangels twice; herald once; and Angel of the Lord once; with another 25 uses of various heavenly hosts. Of the same 304 different songs, 71 contained a reference to Satan or demons, a total of 96 different times, with Satan being used 51 times; foe(s) 18 times; tempter 10 times; hosts of night, hell, evil, wrong once each; powers of darkness, hell, evil once each; devil 3 times; serpent twice; fowler twice; and prince of darkness, evil one, and accuser once each. Thirty-three different writers were responsible for two or more of the compositions containing these references to demonology or angelology, while 162 other writers

had one hymn or song that included such references. Not surprisingly, Charles Wesley led all writers with 13 songs that used one or both of these categories of reference, while John W. Peterson wrote 9 and Fanny Crosby 7.

126. C. S. Lewis, *The Screwtape Letters* (New York: Macmillan, 1948), p. 39.

127. Ibid., p. 9.

*Teaching Helps*

## *Outline for Teaching*

I. Angelology

- A. Definition and Delineation of the Subject
- B. Scriptural Names, Terms, and References Considered
- C. Angels in the Old Testament
    1. The Angel of the Theophany
    2. The nature, appearance, and function of angels
    3. The order, rank, and organization of angels
- D. Angels in the New Testament
    1. Their existence and appearance
    2. The teaching of Jesus concerning angels
    3. The teaching of the epistles and the Book of Revelation
- E. The Development of a Doctrine of Angelology
- F. The View of John Wesley
- G. Guardian Angels
- H. A Summary of Angelology for Contemporary Consideration

II. Demonology

- A. Definition and Delineation of the Subject
- B. Scriptural Names, Terms, and References Considered
- C. The Devil — Satan
    1. The original nature, state, and character of Satan
    2. The fall, moral character, and personality of Satan
    3. The position, power, and destiny of Satan
- D. The Relationship of Fallen Angels to Demons and Evil Spirits
- E. Demon Worship and Demon Possession

F. The Development of a Doctrine of Demonology

1. The origin of Old Testament demonology
2. New Testament demonology
3. The works and kingdom of Satan
4. Beliefs and teachings about Satan and demons through the ages

## *Questions for Discussion*

1. Using Genesis 16, Exodus 3, and Judges 13 as beginning chapters where *malak* and *Yahweh* are used together (as "angel of the Lord"), study as many other passages where this phrase is found in those Bible books and conclude which passages clearly seem to be theophanies.
2. What is the difference between a Theophany and a Christophany? Base your conclusion on data supported by both biblical and theological references.
3. Read from as many commentaries as are available to you concerning the meanings of Genesis 6:2; Job 1:6; 2:1; 38:7. Does the data found support the conclusions projected in this chapter? Where does the weight of evidence lie?
4. Is it proper or improper to refer to angels, demons, or Satan as persons or as possessing personality? Why? Does personhood/personality rest on the basis of corporeity?
5. In what way are members of the human family superior or inferior to the angels? Are there any bases in Scripture for you to believe that the status of angels or of human persons may be subject to change?
6. If in the human family rationality — the thought processes and intelligence — centers in the physical brain, how is it possible for purely spiritual beings, without corporeity, to have such qualities?
7. Using data from biblical and theological resources, work out a reasonable and logical ranking, ordering, and organization of angelic beings.
8. Study all of the New Testament references to any angelic appearance, either to individuals or groups of people, and record the emotional reaction or response to such appearances. What different reactions or responses are found?
9. Make a list of all the various names used of Satan in the Bible and define each Hebrew or Greek word by use of a dictionary and by checking the translation of the same names in at least six different modern translations of the Bible. Compare and contrast three different names of Satan with the names for Persons of the Trinity — God the Father, the Son, and the Holy Spirit.
10. How is it possible to distinguish clearly between devils and demons? Is such distinction imperative? Why or why not?

11. What is the difference between the terms *exorcism* and *expulsion?* Were Christ and His disciples/apostles exorcists? What can be said for or against using the terms interchangeably?
12. Is there a difference between "demon possession" and "demon oppression"? Can a Christian believer, who is Spirit-led and Spirit-filled be demon possessed at the same time? Is all demon possession voluntary?

# *Recommendations for Further Reading*


## I. Angelology

Carter, Charles W., and Earle, Ralph. *The Acts of the Apostles* (Grand Rapids: Zondervan, 1973),pp. 149-50.

Fitzwater, P. B. *Christian Theology* (Grand Rapids: Eerdmans, 1948), pp. 250-59.

Knight, George A. F. *A Christian Theology of the Old Testament* (Richmond, Va.: John Knox, 1959), pp. 68-83, 127-39.

Miley, John. *Systematic Theology* (New York: The Methodist Book Concern, 1894), 2:490-504.

Sheldon, Henry C. *System of Christian Doctrine* (Cincinnati: Jennings & Graham, 1903), pp. 257-71.

Thiessen, Henry C. *Introductory Lectures in Systematic Theology* (Grand Rapids: Eerdmans, 1977), pp. 190-212.

Wright, J. Stafford. *Man in the Process of Time*, (Grand Rapids: Eerdmans, 1956), chapter entitled "Man and His Unseen Neighbors," pp. 123-37.

## II. Demonology

Alexander, William M. *Demonic Possession in the New Testament* (Grand Rapids: Baker 1980), pp. 1-284.

Bounds, Edward M. *Satan: His Personality, Power and Overthrow* (New York: Revell, 1922), pp. 11-157.

Chafer, Lewis Sperry. *Satan, His Motive and Methods* (Grand Rapids: Zondervan, 1977), pp. 15-134.

*Demon Experiences in Many Lands*, compiled by Kenneth N. Taylor (Chicago: Moody, 1960), pp. 11-128.

Montgomery, John Warwick, ed. *Demon Possession* (Minneapolis: Bethany Fellowship, 1956), pp. 29-371.

Needham, Mrs. George C. *Angels and Demons* (Chicago: Moody, 1963), pp. 47-125.

Pentecost, J. Dwight, *Your Adversary, The Devil* (Grand Rapids: Zondervan, 1976), pp. 11-191.

Philpott, Kent. *A Manual of Demonology and the Occult* (Grand Rapids: Zondervan, 1976), pp. 15-149.

Unger, Merritt F. *Biblical Demonology* (Wheaton, Ill.: Scripture Press, 1963), pp. 1-227.

Wesley, John. *The Works of the Rev. John Wesley* (London: John Mason, 1841), 6:350-60.

# *Bibliography*

## Books

Alexander, William M. *Demonic Possession in the New Testament: Its Historical, Medical and Theological Aspects*. Grand Rapids: Baker 1980.

Bounds, Edward M. *Satan: His Personality, Power and Overthrow*. New York: Revell, 1922

Bultmann, Rudolf. *Kerygma and Myth, A Theological Debate*. New York: Harper and Row, 1961.

Caie, Norman Macleod. *The Seven Deadly Sins*. New York: Doran, 1923.

Chafer, Lewis Sperry. *Satan*. Chicago: Bible Institute Colportage Association, 1935.

______. *Satan, His Motive and Methods*. Grand Rapids: Zondervan, 1977.

Corte, Nicholas. *Who Is the Devil?* New York: Hawthorn, 1958.

Cullman, Oscar. *Christ and Time*. Philadelphia: Westminster, 1964.

Davies, T. Witton. *Magic, Divinations, and Demonology Among the Hebrews and Their Neighbors*. London: James Clarke, 1898.

DeHaan, Richard W. *Satan, Satanism and Witchcraft*. Grand Rapids: Zondervan, 1972.

*Demon Experiences in Many Lands*, compiled by Kenneth N. Taylor. Chicago: Moody, 1960.

Denney, James. *Jesus and the Gospels*. London: Hodder and Stoughton, 1908.

Dickason, C. Fred. *Angels, Elect and Evil*. Chicago: Moody, 1975.

Ebon, Martin, ed., *Satan Trap: Dangers of the Occult*. Garden City, N. Y.: Doubleday, 1976.

Ewen, C. L'Estrange. *Witchcraft and Demonism*. London: Heath Cranton, 1933.

Garcon, Maurice, and Vinchon, Jean. *The Devil*. New York: Dutton, 1930.

Graham, William F. *Angels: God's Secret Agents*. Garden City, N. Y.: Doubleday, 1975.

Gray, James M. *Satan and the Saint*. Chicago: Bible Institute Colportage Association. 1909.

Hume, Robert E. *The World's Leading Religions*. New York: Scribner, 1952.

Jarrel, W. A. *The Devil*. Dallas: Published by the author, 1908.

Kluger, Rinkah S. *Satan in the Old Testament*. Evanston, Ill.: Northwestern University Press, 1967.

Langton, Edward, *Essentials of Demonology*. London: Epworth, 1949.

______. *Good and Evil Spirits*. London: SPCK, 1942.

______. *Satan, A Portrait: A Study of the Character of Satan Through All the Ages*. London: Skeffington, n.d.

Lewis, C. S. *The Screwtape Letters*. New York: Macmillan, 1948.

Lindsey, Hal. *Satan Is Alive and Well on Planet Earth*. Grand Rapids: Zondervan, 1972.

Lovett, C. S. *Dealing With the Devil*. Baldwin Park, Calif.: Personal Christianity, 1967.

______. *Teach Them About Satan*. Baldwin Park, Calif.: Personal Christianity, 1970.

Lyons, Arthur. *The Second Coming: Satanism in America*. New York: Dodd, Meade, 1970.

McRae, Thaddeus. *Lectures on Satan*. Boston: Gould and Lincoln, 1871.

Maple, Eric. *The Domain of Devils*. New York: Barnes, 1966.

Montgomery, John Warwick, ed. *Demon Possession, A Medical, Historical, Anthropological and Theological Symposium*. Minneapolis: Bethany Fellowship, 1976.

Needham, Mrs. George C. *Angels and Demons*. Chicago: Moody, 1963.

Nevius, John L. *Demon Possession*. Grand Rapids: Kregel, 1968.

Pentecost, J. Dwight. *Your Adversary the Devil*. Grand Rapids: Zondervan, 1969.

Peterson, Robert. *Are Demons for Real?* Chicago: Moody, n.d.

Philpott, Kent. *A Manual of Demonology and the Occult*. Grand Rapids: Zondervan, 1973.

Regamey, Pie-Raymond. *What Is an Angel?* Translated from French by Mark Pontifex. New York: Hawthorn, 1950.

Rhodes, H. T. F. *The Satanic Mass*. Hackensack, N. J.: Wehman, 1968.

*Satan*, a composite of translated works by various authors. New York: Sheed and Ward, 1952.

Schwarze, C. Theodore. *The Program of Satan: A Study of the Purpose and Method of the Adversary*. Chicago: Good News, 1947.

Simmons, James P. *War in Heaven*. Cincinnati: Clarke, 1871.

Summers, Montague. *The History of Witchcraft and Demonology*. London: Routledge and Kegan Paul, 1965.

Unger, Merrill F. *Biblical Demonology: A Study of the Spiritual Forces Behind the Present World Unrest*. Wheaton, Ill.: Scripture Press, 1963.

______. *Demons in the World Today*. Wheaton, Ill.: Tyndale, 1971.

Ward, Theodora. *Men and Angels*. New York: Viking, 1969.

Wimberly, C. F. *Is the Devil a Myth?* Cincinnati: God's Revivalist Office, 1913.

Withrow, W. H. *The Spirit World*. New York: Revell, 1906.

Wright, J. Stafford. *Man in the Process of Time*. Grand Rapids: Eerdmans, 1956.

**Commentaries and Theological Works**

*Anchor Bible*, 44 vols. Garden City, N. Y.: Doubleday, 1964.

Aquinas, Thomas, *Summa Theologica*. New York: McGraw Hill, 1970. Vols 1, 15.

*Beacon Bible Commentary*, 10 vols. Kansas City, Mo.: Beacon Hill, 1974.

Berkouwer, G. C. "Satan and Demons." In *Basic Christian Doctrines*. Edited by Carl F. H. Henry. Grand Rapids: Baker, 1973.

Brown, William Adams. *Christian Theology in Outline*. New York: Scribner, 1912.

Calvin, John. A *Compend of the Institutes of the Christian Religion*, Edited by Hugh T. Kerr, Jr. Philadelphia: Presbyterian Board of Christian Education, 1939.

______. *Institutes of the Christian Religion*. 2 vols. Edited by John T. McNeill, Philadelphia: Westminster, 1960.

Carter, Charles W., ed. *Wesleyan Bible Commentary*. 7 vols. Grand Rapids: Eerdmans, 1967.

Carter, Charles W., and Earle, Ralph. *The Acts of the Apostles*. Grand Rapids: Zondervan, 1973.

Clarke, Adam. A *Commentary and Critical Notes*. 6 vols. New York: Abingdon-Cokesbury, n.d.

Clarke, William Newton. *An Outline of Christian Theology*. New York: Scribner, 1917.

Dale, R. W. *Christian Doctrine*. London: Hodder and Stoughton, 1894.

Davidson, A. B. *The Book of Job*. Edinburgh: Williams and Norgate, 1862.

______. *Theology of the Old Testament*. New York: Scribner, 1906.

Driver, Samuel R. *The Book of Job*. Oxford: Clarendon, 1906.

Ewald, Heinrick. *Old and New Testament Theology*. Edinburgh: T. & T. Clark, 1888.

Fitzwater, P. B. *Christian Theology: A Systematic Presentation*. Grand Rapids: Eerdmans, 1948.

Godet, F. *Studies in the Old Testament*. London: Hodder and Stoughton, 1892.

Keil, C. F., and Delitzsch, F. *Biblical Commentary on the Old Testament*. Grand Rapids: Eerdmans, 1971.

Knight, George A. F. A *Christian Theology of the Old Testament*. Richmond, Va.: John Knox, 1959.

Knudson, Albert C. *The Religious Thinking of the Old Testament*. New York: Abingdon, 1918.

Kohler, K. *Jewish Theology*. New York: Macmillan, 1923.

Lange, Peter. *Commentary on the Holy Scriptures: Critical, Doctrinal, and Homiletical*. Grand Rapids: Zondervan, n.d.

Lee, Luther. *Elements of Theology, or an Explanation of the Origin Doctrines, Morals and Institutions of Christianity*. Syracuse, N. Y.: A. W. Hall, 1899.

Martensen, H. *Christian Dogmatics: A Compendium of the Doctrines of Christianity*. Edinburgh: T. & T. Clark, 1878.

Miley, John. *Systematic Theology*. 2 vols. New York: Hunt and Eaton, 1894.

Mullins, Edgar Y. *The Christian Religion in Its Doctrinal Expression*. Philadelphia: Roger Williams, 1917.

Oehler, Gustav Friedrich. *Theology of the Old Testament*. New York: Funk & Wagnalls, 1885.

Purkiser, W. T.; Taylor, Richard S.; and Taylor, Willard H. *God, Man and Salvation*. Kansas City, Mo.: Beacon Hill, 1977.

Ramm, Bernard. "Angels." In *Basic Christian Doctrines*. Edited by Carl F. H. Henry. GrandRapids: Baker, 1973.

Sheldon, H. C. *New Testament Theology*. New York: Macmillan, 1911.

______. *System of Christian Doctrine*. Cincinnati: Jennings and Graham, 1903.

Shultz, Hermann. *Old Testament Theology*. Edinburgh: T. & T. Clark, 1909. Vol. 2.

Stevens, George Barker. *The Theology of the New Testament*. New York: Scribner, 1911.

Thielicke, Helmut. *The Evangelical Faith*. Translated and edited by Geoffrey W. Bromiley. Grand Rapids: Eerdmans, 1977.

Thiessen, Henry C. *Introductory Lectures in Systematic Theology*. Grand Rapids: Eerdmans, 1977.

Wesley, John. *Explanatory Notes Upon the New Testament*. Salem, Ohio: Schmul, 1975.

______. *Explanatory Notes Upon the Old Testament*. 3 vols. Salem, Ohio: Schmul, 1975.

______. *The Works of the Rev. John Wesley*. London: John Mason, 1840.

Wiley, H. Orton. *Christian Theology*. 3 vols. Kansas City, Mo.: Beacon Hill, 1945.

Wiley, H. Orton, and Culbertson, Paul T. *Introduction to Christian Theology*. Kansas City, Mo.: Beacon Hill, 1946.

Young, Edward J. *The Prophecy of Daniel*. Grand Rapids: Eerdmans, 1949.

## ***Dictionaries, Encyclopaedias, and Other Reference Works***

Barton, George A. "Demons and Spirits," In *Hastings Encyclopaedia of Religion and Ethics*. Edited by James Hastings. 12 vols. New York: Scribner, 1914. Vol. 4.

Blau, Ludwig. "Satan." In *The Jewish Encyclopaedia*. New York: Funk & Wagnalls, 1909. Vol. 9.

Breward, Ian. "Witchcraft." In *New International Dictionary of the Christian Church*. Edited by J. D. Douglas. Grand Rapids: Zondervan, 1974.

Bromiley, Geoffrey W. "Angel." In *Baker's Dictionary of Theology*. Edited by E. Harrison. Grand Rapids: Baker, 1960.

*Complete Works of Flavius Josephus*. 10 Vols. New York: World Syndicate, n.d.

*Concise Oxford Dictionary of the Christian Church*. Edited by Elizabeth A. Livingstone. London: Oxford University Press, 1977.

Gilmore, George W. "Demon, Demonism." In *The New Schaff-Herzog Encyclopaedia of Religious Knowledge*. Edited by Samuel Macauley Jackson. New York: Funk & Wagnalls, 1909.

Hobart, William Kirk. *The Medical Language of St. Luke*. Grand Rapids: Baker, 1954.

Loewe, Herbert. "Demons and Spirits." In *Jewish Encyclopaedia of Religion and Ethics*. Editedby James Hastings. New York: Scribner, 1914. Vol. 4.

M'Clintock, John, and Strong, James, eds. *Cyclopaedia of Biblical, Theological and Ecclesiastical Literature*. 12 Vols. New York: Harper and Brothers, 1895. Vols. 2, 9.

Meagher, Paul K.; O'Brien, Thomas C.; and Aherne, Consuelo M., eds. *Encyclopaedic Dictionary of Religion*. Washington, D. C.: Corpus, 1979. Vols. 1-3.

Milton, John. "Paradise Lost." In *The Harvard Classics*. Edited by Charles W. Eliot. New York: Collier, 1909.

Schaff, D. S. "Devil." In *The New Schaff-Herzog Encyclopaedia of Religious Knowledge*. Editedby Samuel Macauley Jackson. New York: Funk and Wagnalls, 1909. Vol. 3.

Stewart, Roy A. "Angel." In *New International Dictionary of the Christian Church*. Edited by J. D. Douglas. Grand Rapids: Zondervan, 1974.

Sweet, Louis Matthew. "Demon." In *International Standard Bible Encyclopaedia*. Edited by James Orr. Grand Rapids: Eerdmans, 1947. Vol. 2.

______. "Satan." In *International Standard Bible Encyclopaedia*. Edited by James Orr. 5 vols. Grand Rapids: Eerdmans, 1947, Vol. 4.

Unger, Merrill F. "Demon." In *Baker's Dictionary of the Bible*. Grand Rapids: Baker, n.d.

Vincent, Marvin R. *Word Studies in the New Testament*. 4 vols. Grand Rapids: Eerdmans, 1946. Vol. 3.

Wilson, John MacCartney. "Angel." In *International Standard Bible Encyclopaedia*. Edited by James Orr. 5 vols. Grand Rapids: Eerdmans, 1947. Vol. 1.

Young, Robert. *Analytical Concordance to the Bible*. New York: Funk and Wagnalls, n.d.

***Periodicals***

Allen, R. L. "Lucifer, Who or What?" *Journal of the Evangelical Society* 11 (Winter 1968): 35ff.

Barnhouse, D. G. "Invisible War," *Eternity*, in 6 parts, 7-12 (January - June 1956): 24ff; 22ff; 20ff; 22ff; 18ff; 20ff.

Bechtel, P. "Witches in the Air," *Christian Life* 29 (March 1968): 40ff.

Bell, L. M. "The Dreadful Reality of Satan," *Christianity Today* (October 15, 1957), p. 18.

Bellshaw, W. G. "New Testament Doctrine of Satan," *Grace Journal* 9 (Fall 1968): 24-39.

Berkouwer, G. C. "Satan and the Demons," *Christianity Today* (June 5, 1961), pp. 18ff.

Breese, David. "The Devil Says It's So," *Moody Monthly* 74 (June 1974): 36ff.

Buher, R. B. "Are the demons Real Today?" *Christian Life* 29 (March 1968): 42ff.

Chambers, Wittaker. "The Devil," *Life* (February 2, 1948), pp. 84-85.

Climenhaga, A. M. "Is Jesus' Return Indicated by the Rise of the Occult?" *Christian Life* 39 (April 1970): 9-12.

"Demon Power Today" (editorial), *Christian Life* 20 (June 1958): 14-16.

Gotoas, D. S. "Spirits, Mediums and the Witch of Endor." *Moody Monthly* 68 (March 1968): 37-38.

Graham, William F. "Did the Devil Make You Do It?" *Decision* 14 (October 1973): 1-2.

Harris, L. "One View of Demon Possession," *His* 35 (March 1975): 9-10.

Jackson, B., and Vincent, M. O. "Two Doctors Respond to Harris," *His* (March 1975): 11.

Kucharsky, David. "Graham on Demons," *Christianity Today* (June 7, 1974), pp. 49-50.

Kuhn, Harold B. "Providence? Or the Age of Aquarius?" *Christianity Today* (June 20, 1969), p. 39.

Lindsey, Hal. "New Age of Satan — Are You Prepared?" *Moody Monthly* 73 (April 1973): 96-102.

Lockyer, Herbert. "The Angels and Judgements," *The Sunday School Times and Gospel Herald* (December 1, 1976), pp. 12-13.

______. "The Lord of the Angels," *The Sunday School Times and Gospel Herald* (December 15, 1976), pp. 12-13.

McElhern, C. K. "You Can Claim the Power of God," *Christian Life* 27 (March 1966): 44-45.

McKenna, David L. "Man and Devil Today," *United Evangelical Action* 33 (Summer 1974): 6-7.

Meade, R. J. "Demon Activity Today," *Christian Life* 23 (February 1962): 38-41.

______. "Unclean Spirits: Your Questions Answered," *Christian Life* 24 (May 1962): 28ff.

______. "Who Is Satan?" *Christian Life* 23 (January 1962): 30ff.

Olson, Norman A. "Angels: Where Do They Come From? What Do They Do?" *Good News Broadcaster* 36 (September 1978): 16-17.

Pelikan, J. "Angel and Evangel," *Concordia Theological Monthly* 45 (January 1974): 4-7.

Ramm, Bernard. "Angels," *Christianity Today* (May 22, 1961), pp. 18-19.

Smith, C. R. "The New Testament Doctrine of Demons," *Grace Journal* 10 (Spring 1969): 26-42.

Smith, W. M. "Angels: Heaven's Inhabitants," *Eternity* 27 (December 1976): 61ff.

Taylor, A., and Beausay, W. "Angels in Your Life," *Christian Life* 37 (May 1975): 28-29.

Unger, Merrill F. "Old Testament Revelation of the Creation of Angels and the Earth," *Bibliotheca Sacra* 114 (July 1957): 206-12.

______. "Old Testament Revelation of Eternity Past," *Bibliotheca Sacra* 114 (April 1957): 133-40.

Wisdom, T. "Cherubim," *Biblical Viewpoint* 10 (November 1976): 124-32.

Woodrum, Lon. "What About Devils?" *United Evangelical Action* 22 (May 1963): 98ff.

Young, W. "Demons Today," *Moody Monthly* 56 (May 1956): 20ff.

***Bible Versions***

King James Version of the Holy Bible, New Encyclopaedic Reference Edition. Grand Rapids: Zondervan, 1966.

New American Standard Bible. The Lockman Foundation. New York: Thomas Nelson, 1977.

New International Version. Grand Rapids: Zondervan. Copyright 1978, New York International Bible Society.

Revised Standard Version. *The New Oxford Annotated Bible With the Apocrypha*. New York: Oxford University Press, 1977.

*Zondervan Parallel New Testament in Greek and English*. Grand Rapids: Zondervan. Copyright 1975. The Iversen-Norman Associates.

***Unpublished Theses***

Caldwell, Wayne E. "The Concept of Satan in Biblical Literature," a thesis presented to the faculty of Central Baptist Theological Seminary, Kansas City, Kansas, for degree of Master of Theology, May 1957.

Carter, Charles W. "The Validity of the Concept of Soul as Shown by Animistic and Ancient Thought," a thesis presented to the faculty of the School of Religion, Butler University, Indianapolis, Indiana, for degree of Master of Theology, 1950.

Loong, Titus. "Evidences for Psycho-Physical Disorders and Their Remedies in the Gospels and Acts." a thesis presented to the faculty of China Evangelical Seminary, Charles W. Carter, Adviser, for degree of Master of Divinity, May 1974.

Sheridan, Lois E. (Ellis). "Magic and Its Influence on Primitive Medicine," a thesis presented to the faculty of Marion College, Marion, Indiana, Charles W. Carter, Adviser, for degree of Master of Religion, 1950.

*About the Author…*

WAYNE E. CALDWELL IS Professor of Theology at Marion College. He earned his Th.M. degree at Central Baptist Theological Seminary and his Th.D. degree at Iliff School of Theology in Denver. He has served as a pastor to various churches in the Kansas Conference of the Wesleyan Methodist Church and has been an evangelistic speaker at nearly two hundred revivals, crusades, Bible conferences, and other meetings.

Dr. Caldwell has co-authored another book published by Schmul Publishing Company entitled *The Genius of the New Testament Church*. As well, he has contributed numerous articles to the Wesleyan Methodist Church and the Wesleyan Church periodicals since 1949. He is a member of the American Council of the Blind; the American Council of the Blind of Indiana; and the Grant County, Indiana, Services for the Blind. He is a member of the Wesleyan Theological Society, having served as secretary-treasurer of the society.